D1480876   UM

Donated by

PATRICIA PHILLIPS MARCO

TREES FOR TOWN & COUNTRY

'Tree with Ivy', 1978, by Henry Moore, OM, CH

TREES
FOR TOWN & COUNTRY
A PRACTICAL GUIDE TO PLANTING & CARE

Peter Bridgeman, NDH, ND Arb

With line drawings by Margaret Bridgeman, NDD

David & Charles
NEWTON ABBOT   LONDON   NORTH POMFRET (Vt)

To Leonie, Michael and Daniel

British Library Cataloguing in Publication Data

Bridgeman, Peter Harry
  Trees for town and country.
  1. Tree planting – Great Britain
  2. Trees, Care of – Great Britain
  I. Title
  634.9'5   SB435

  ISBN 0–7153–7841–4

© Peter Bridgeman, P. J. Jordan and M. J. Whitehead 1979

All rights reserved. No part of this
publication may be reproduced, stored
in a retrieval system, or transmitted,
in any form or by any means, electronic,
mechanical, photocopying, recording or
otherwise, without the prior permission
of David & Charles (Publishers) Limited

Typeset by Northern Phototypesetting Co., Bolton
and printed in Great Britain
by Redwood Burn Ltd., Trowbridge, Wiltshire
for David & Charles (Publishers) Limited
Brunel House Newton Abbot Devon

Published in the United States of America
by David & Charles Inc.
North Pomfret Vermont 05053 USA

Contents

Acknowledgements

The author acknowledges with thanks the assistance of Mr M. John Whitehead for the preparation of the Classification and Naming of Trees chapter and the Tree Directory, Mrs Pamela Jordan for the Tree Growth chapter and Dr Keith Lever for his advice on the chapter concerning Tree Disorders.

He also wishes to thank his sister-in-law, Mrs Margaret Bridgeman, NDD, for the artwork and his wife, Leonie Bridgeman, for typing the manuscript.

Finally, he is particularly grateful to Mr Henry Moore for his permission to reproduce his drawing 'Tree with Ivy' as the frontispiece.

All photographs are by the author with the exception of plates 57–66 and plate 69, which were kindly loaned by the Forestry Commission and remain their copyright.

Introduction

Britain is very fortunate in that with its geographical situation, temperate climate and range of soil types it can successfully grow a vast range of trees. Only some thirty-five species are truly native (that is, they were growing in this country before it broke away from the continent about six thousand years ago), e.g. oak, ash, beech, birch, pine. Others such as sweet and horse chestnut, walnut and sycamore have been introduced from Europe over the centuries and are accepted now as near natives, harmonising well in our British landscape. Still more have been imported from other parts of the world in the last two or three centuries and are classed as exotic. These exotic species have richly improved our range of trees in arboreta, parks and gardens, but some look out of place and foreign in the rural countryside.

Whatever their origins, this great wealth of trees has formed a vital part of our town and country landscape. However, comparatively little amenity planting has been carried out this century and, because of disease, adverse weather conditions, modern farming methods, new roads and housing development, much of our tree cover has been severely depleted.

It has been estimated that in England and Wales alone over fifty million trees have been lost in the past twenty-five years. Dutch elm disease, the greatest single disaster, has already killed over fifteen million trees. The droughts of 1975–6 not only resulted in the loss of thousands of young transplants through lack of water but many thousands of acres of woodlands and plantations were destroyed by fire; every year storms and gales uproot thousands of trees.

In order to be economic, modern farming methods require larger field sizes and consequently many thousands of miles of hedgerows have been removed. It also appears cheaper to burn straw and stubble rather than to utilise it and, unless this is carefully controlled, hedgerows, trees and wildlife habitats can be destroyed.

A six-lane motorway takes up twenty-five acres per mile and up to forty thousand acres of agricultural land are lost each year to building. The increase in building land values has resulted in more houses per acre and, therefore, more trees have to be felled.

Owing to one or more of these factors many areas are now virtually treeless, or only old over-mature and often dangerous trees remain. The 'Plant a Tree in '73' campaign helped create a public awareness that Britain's trees are in peril, while government departments and many local authorities are very conscious of the problems and are successfully protecting and planting trees. However, there remains much ignorance, apathy and waste of money by ill-conceived maintenance and planting schemes.

This practical guide is intended to inform and instruct those who own land or are responsible for our landscape, as well as individual householders who, by not felling or lopping one tree or by planting another, can do so much to help.

Much of the selection, planting and small tree maintenance can be carried out by the keen do-it-yourselfer. However, many of the large tree-work operations are potentially very dangerous and, unless the 'amateur' is properly trained and equipped, are best carried out by professionals.

Where it has not been possible to cover certain subjects in depth the reader is referred to specialist books or sources of further advice.

The landowners and planters of the eighteenth and nineteenth centuries created today's mature tree cover – we are neglecting it. We inherited a beautiful and varied landscape and collectively we must ensure that there will be an acceptable living and working environment for the twenty-first century. Future generations will thank us if we do and rightly condemn us if we do not.

1 A Brief History of Arboriculture in the British Isles

Most of Britain's existing landscape is man-made or has been influenced by man's activities. This has been a slow and gradual process over the past few thousand years but greatly accelerated since the seventeenth century and particularly in the last twenty-five years.

As the weather conditions improved after the last Ice Age, trees slowly invaded and colonised the land. Probably birch and pine were the early pioneer species followed by oak, ash and alder as the conditions improved further. Before Britain separated from the main continent of Europe, trees such as beech, lime, holly, yew and thorns had become established. It is likely that thirty-five species were growing naturally at that time and that at one point some 60 per cent of the land surface was covered by trees. Without man's interference it would be very similar today, with large trees dominating the landscape and forming huge forests interrupted only by water and the highest mountains.

The early Britons were hunters and fishermen and practised no agriculture but as man progressed, settled and developed communities so his influence on the natural tree cover increased. Trees provided wood for housing, weapons, fuel and early forms of transport, and their fruit and seed were food for both man and animal. The effect of this was minimal as new young trees would soon replace those lost. The developments in agriculture, however, resulted in larger areas being cleared to create fields and grazing animals prevented natural regeneration by eating the young seedlings.

The Romans accelerated the process by more advanced technology and by constructing straight roads that required tree removal, rather than following natural paths around the trees and contours. Probably to their credit the Romans also introduced new species of trees such as the sweet chestnut and the walnut.

Apparently the Saxon kings introduced forest laws to protect royal hunting grounds but the first real statutes were passed by the Normans, who again were anxious to protect their hunting areas: any person taking the king's deer, for example, was punished by death. The necessity to impose such harsh rules must have meant that the woodland cover was in decline, but these royal forests accounted for only a small percentage of the total land area and the erosion of the tree cover continued.

As man developed further he found more and more uses for tree products. Charcoal burners required vast volumes of small-sized trees for smelting metals or making glass. Fencing was an important industry and this again required small-diameter trees for hurdles and posts. Timber was the main material for house and bridge constructon and for furniture and farm implements.

Since all the felling was carried out by hand, with no mechanical equipment, the smaller young trees were selected, leaving the old large specimens. This resulted in an age/size imbalance and the process of natural regeneration of our woodlands was affected.

The regular cutting of some small trees resulted in vigorous regrowth of shoots from the base and coppice woods were thus formed to provide a regular supply of small timber.

Wooden ships required larger trees. Huge open-crown oaks were felled to provide timber for the hulls, and many thousands of trees would be required to construct a large man-o'-war.

Early forest protection, as mentioned, was mainly for preserving hunting rights, but by the seventeenth century the effect of this large-scale felling was causing more widespread concern. One man who was acutely aware of the problem was John Evelyn, the diarist and court officer to Charles I and Charles II. Following a lecture to the Royal Society he published in 1664 his famous book *Silva, or a Discourse of Forest Trees, and the Propagation of Timber in his Majesty's Dominions.* The main reason for this work was anxiety over the shortage of timber for shipbuilding, but also he realised the value of a sustained supply of timber for more general purposes and amenity. From this time landowners began planting trees as a crop, and forestry as we know it today was established.

Landowners also began to enclose their land within defined boundaries and the Enclosure Acts set the pattern of hedgerows and boundaries that still exists today. An artificial landscape was emerging, with the intensive stocking of fenced-in fields resulting in permanent pastures where no tree seedlings could survive.

Sixteenth- and seventeenth-century travellers

were introducing more and more species of trees to this country: from the Old World the horse chestnut and the cedar of Lebanon, and from the New World the Robinia, tulip tree, swamp cypress and Thuya. By the eighteenth century plant hunters were travelling to the far corners of the world and sending back seeds of many more exotic trees. Large landowners began to landscape their estates and arboreta were created to house these new introductions. Lord Weymouth planted so many white pines at Longleat that they named the tree after him. The Duke of Atholl planted millions of trees, many of them larch from Europe, in the Perthshire highlands. Famous landscapers such as Kent, Bridgeman, 'Capability' Brown and Humphrey Repton used both the indigenous and the introduced trees to frame their designs. Many of their famous gardens survive today, though the trees are at or past maturity.

Establishments and organisations such as Kew and the Horticultural Society and early nurseries such as Veitch & Sons sponsored further plant-hunting expeditions. David Douglas explored the west coast of America, particularly the Columbia River area where he collected seeds of many important new pine species and the Douglas fir. Other famous collectors followed in his footsteps: Thomas Nuttall (*Cornus nuttallii*), Hartweg (redwoods and Monterey cypress), John Jeffrey (western hemlock) and William Lobb (western red cedar, Wellingtonia, and from South America the Chile pine). Others travelled to the Far East. Sir Joseph Hooker collected Rhododendrons, birch and Magnolias from the Himalayas and India. Robert Fortune introduced umbrella pine and Cryptomeria from Japan. William Kerr (junipers and Kerria) began to show the vast range of trees and shrubs that were growing in China. Later Robert Fortune, Reginald Farrer and, probably the most important collector in the East, Ernest Henry 'Chinese' Wilson explored the hidden depths of China. Wilson in four journeys introduced a wide variety of trees and shrubs including maples, Magnolia, Rhododendrons and dogwoods. The great range of trees and shrubs which is now available in this country can be attributed to these early pioneers who risked suffering and sometimes death to find, collect and dispatch their treasures.

As the arboreta and large private estates revelled in this new-found wealth of plants the rest of the landscape was still suffering from the effects of increasing human activity. The industrial revolution introduced mechanisation in agriculture and the growth of industrial towns.

More land was required for housing, roads and farming; more trees had to go.

By the end of the nineteenth century the recently formed local authorities were planting trees in towns and urban parks. Much good work was carried out and our city parks today show the results of imaginative planting schemes and bold avenue planting. However, some of the street planting was controlled by over-zealous and often inadequately trained staff and many of our towns still face the problems of huge forest trees in small streets which require expensive and ugly lopping to control their size.

The inadequacy of forestry planting in the nineteenth century was highlighted by World War I, when timber imports were restricted and the home producers could not meet demands. In 1919 the Forestry Commission was established with the primary function of developing forestry to provide a future supply of timber.

Tree planting and care can be directly related to the economic situation and, therefore, very little amenity planting was carried out between the wars. With the improved economy and increasing home ownership of the 1950s, trees again were being planted by local authorities and small private householders. Many of our towns were greatly improved by tree planting but in the country areas trees were being removed at a far greater rate in the name of farm efficiency and economy. New roads, particularly motorways, were being cut through the countryside and new towns swallowed up thousands of acres. The large rich estates which had planted so many trees in the nineteenth century were feeling the effects of inflation and many great tree collections were over-maturing and in decline. New and improved legislation was introduced to protect important trees but the escalating land values resulted in more houses per acre, therefore fewer trees could be retained.

By the 1960s many professionals were concerned about loss of trees and poor standards of workmanship, and two new professionally-based tree societies were formed. The Arboricultural Association and the Association of British Tree Surgeons and Arborists were established in 1964 with similar objectives of improving tree care and raising standards of workmanship. The Royal Forestry Society introduced examinations in arboriculture so that staff with knowledge and experience could be recognised by qualifications. Later, in 1968, the first full-time educational course in arboriculture was established at Merrist Wood Agricultural College.

The late 1960s also saw the advent of the worst

single disaster to affect our tree cover. A new virulent strain of Dutch elm disease had been imported on timber from North America. Before it was realised that the disease was this fatal, aggressive strain, it had spread throughout the southern half of England and in the next ten years over fifteen million elms were to die.

It has been estimated that because of disease, adverse weather, new building developments and hedgerow removal, over fifty million trees have been lost in the past twenty-five years. The government for its part has been fully aware of this situation and in 1974 helped form The Tree Council. This council acts as a forum for all the organisations concerned with trees and land use and ownership in an attempt to halt the decline in our tree population and to ensure sufficient replanting. Stronger legislation has been introduced to protect trees, and the Countryside Commission, the Forestry Commission and others offer grant aid for tree planting (see Appendix 1, Sources of Advice and Information).

Now there is sufficient goodwill and public concern over our trees, but this must be converted into sound practical schemes, not only to protect our existing trees but also to plant many millions more for the future.

2 Classification and Naming of Trees

M. J. Whitehead, ND Arb, Kew Dip (Hort)

Anyone interested in animals and plants usually becomes absorbed with the infinite variety of their forms, every one of which requires a suitable and separate name. To facilitate communication and understanding throughout the world, Latin has been adopted as being unbiased to any country and is universally accepted as the basis for scientific naming of all life forms. Common vernacular names are useful in their country of origin but as many plants have been introduced from other countries their use is limited and can often be confusing. Latin tags *can* be accepted and used freely, as is evident from such familiar names as hippopotamus, chrysanthemum and magnolia.

With the vast number of species evolved in the world's varied and complex environments, there needs to be a scientifically orderly system of studying, classifying and naming plants so that they may be distinguished and managed for food, breeding trials and various economic and environmental uses in wild, cultivated and built-up areas. The key factor of this management is to arrange all the plants into related groups – the science of taxonomy. The formulation of names is covered by the rules of nomenclature.

Taxonomy

Scientists who are engaged in taxonomy are called taxonomists (derived from *taxis*, a Greek word meaning 'to arrange'). Their work involves classifying groups of plants into a series of categories according to the relationships with one another revealed through various studies of plant evolution. These categories are put into an orderly arrangement called the 'plant kingdom', and constitute what is known as the 'taxonomic hierarchy': the classification of groups by a process of dividing and subdividing according to relationships until the basic botanical unit of species is categorised.

Starting with the two primary divisons of the plant kingdom – Spermatophyta (seed-bearing plants) and Crytograms (spore-bearing plants) – the logical arrangement down to the individual plant species is as set out in the table on p. 12.

For most practical purposes it is only necessary to become familiar with families, genera and species.

Family

The family is an assemblage of groups called genera which often resemble each other in general or specific appearance. For example, conifer families can be placed in order of advancement according to the number of seeds borne on each scale of the fruiting cone: Araucariaceae with one seed per cone scale, Pinaceae with two, Taxodiaceae having up to nine seeds and Cupressaceae having many seeds per cone scale. There are, however, exceptions; for example, *Juniperus monosperma* in the family Cupressaceae has only one seed in each fruit.

It is important to be aware of family grouping as this can have a bearing on tree selection with reference to disease resistance, propagation method etc.

Genus (plural Genera)

Families have their related similar groups allotted into genera, e.g. *Pinus* (pines) or *Quercus* (oaks), each genus having one or more species. The monotypic family Ginkgoaceae has only one genus, *Ginkgo*. A larger family such as Cupressaceae has nineteen genera. There are an estimated 10,000 genera of seed plants (Spermatophyta).

Species

To enable these numerous groups to be managed the genera are further divided into the basic individual botanical unit called species. There are an estimated 250,000 individual species of flowering plants, each requiring a separate name.

The species embraces individual plants which are identical to one another botanically and originate from common parents, their seed producing similar individuals.

Many species names are descriptive: *excelsior*, for example, which is allotted to our native ash tree and added to the generic name to give *Fraxinus excelsior*, means 'taller'. The species name *americana* is added to the same generic name for the related American white ash, *Fraxinus americana*.

Nomenclature

Nomenclature is the process by which plants are named. Problems can occur when taxonomists

PLANT KINGDOM

Primary Division	Class	Sub-Class	Order e.g.	Family e.g.	Genus e.g.	Species	Common English Name
Spermatophyta (seed-bearing plants)	Angiospermae	Monocotyledoneae	Liliales	Amaryllidaceae	Galanthus	nivalis	snowdrop
		Dicotyledoneae	Rosales	Rosaceae	Pyrus	communis	pear tree
	Gymonspermae	Coniferopsida	Coniferales	Pinaceae	Pinus	sylvestris	Scots pine
			Taxales	Taxaceae	Taxus	baccata	yew
			Ginkgoales	Ginkgoaceae	Ginkgo	biloba	maidenhair tree
		Cycadopsida	Cycadales	Cycadaceae	Cycas	revoluta	cycad
			Gnetales	Ephedraceae	Ephedra	major	ephedra
Cryptograms (spore-bearing plants)	Pteridophyta (ferns, horsetails and club mosses)						
	Bryophyta (mosses and liverworts)						
	Thallophyta (fungi and algae)						

and botanists adopt different systems when classifying genera and species. Nature sets no formal boundaries, and authoritative opinion can change with the advancement of time and knowledge.

The eighteenth-century naturalist Linnaeus devised a suitable system of classification. Further research has, however, illustrated over-simplification. For instance, he placed fir, pine, larch and spruce all under the genus *Pinus*, whereas modern scientific studies can prove that these trees deserve their own distinguishable status as genera, i.e. *Abies* (fir), *Pinus* (pine), *Larix* (larch) and *Picea* (spruce). Hence the evolving problems of name changes which continue today.

International Rules of Nomenclature

To help overcome the problem of name changes and to manage scientifically the vast numbers of genera and species, botanical scientists have agreed to international rules. These rules were established in 1867 at an International Botanical Congress in Paris. It was then agreed that all valid or correct names should be dated back to 1735 when Linnaeus devised the binomial system of naming plants by genus and species.

The genus is usually derived as a Latin noun and is used as the first step in tracing plant names, just like finding a person's surname in a directory. The species (specific epithet) is the more informal, individual and often descriptive part of the name.

The rules have been revised and improved in successive International Botanical Congress meetings and are now accepted worldwide as the International Rules for Botanical Nomenclature.

Before the introduction of these rules and the Linnaeus binomial system, botanists adopted lengthy descriptive Latin names: for the American tulip tree, *Liriodendron tulipifera*, for example, they would write *Arbor tulipifera tripartito aceris folio*.

Botanical name changes

The rules, by standardising Latin names, facilitate the use of an orderly system and lessen the risk of confusion. But it is still possible for botanists in separate parts of the world to name the same plant differently, and this may not become evident for many years. If this does occur the rules state that the oldest published name is valid.

To help trace plant names and for reasons of accuracy and completeness the author of the plant name has his own abbreviated name applied to that particular plant, e.g.:

Fagus sylvatica L. (author Linnaeus, 1707–78; Swedish)
Fagus japonica Maxim. (author C. J. Maximowicz, 1827–91; Russian)

Correct form of Latin names

To standardise and identify categories, the botanical rules employ different ways in which to write each part of the plant name. The following rules apply to each part of the name.

Genus
The genus is the first part of the binomial name, constitutes a group of species and is comparable with a person's surname.

The generic name should be written with an initial capital, e.g.:

Pinus (pine)
Quercus (oak)

Species
The species is the second part of the name, and describes individual plants.

The species name should always be written without an initial capital, e.g.:

Pinus sylvestris (Scots pine)
Quercus robur (English oak)

Variety
Widespread species may become isolated, for example by islands or mountain ranges, and evolve into geographic variants which will reproduce true from seed.

Varieties have a third name added to the genus and species, which is written in small letters and has the abbreviation 'var' preceding the variety name, e.g.:

Pinus nigra var *maritima* (Corsican pine)
Cedrus libani var *stenocoma* (Turkish cedar)

The terms 'subspecies' and 'forma' may be used to denote variations within a species.

Hybrids
Hybrids are the result of cross-pollination of two different but related species in the same genus. The new plant has characteristics of both parents and often gives rise to hybrid vigour or pest or disease resistance. Such cross-pollination may occur in the wild or in tree collections or arboreta where exotic trees are planted in close proximity.

Hybrid names are written with small letters and have an 'x' inserted between the generic and the hybrid name, e.g.:

Tilia x *europaea*
(*Tilia cordata* x *T. platyphyllus*)

Bi-generic hybrid

The cross-pollination of two separate but related genera is more uncommon.

The rules indicate the written bi-generic hybrid by placing the '×' at the beginning of the new generic hybrid name, e.g.:

× *Cupressocyparis leylandii*
(*Cupressus macrocarpa* × *Chamaecyparis nootkatensis*)

Cupressus macrocarpa occurs naturally in California and *Chamaecyparis nootkatensis* farther north on the west coast of North America. Therefore in their natural surroundings it is unlikely that these two trees would have ever produced a bi-generic hybrid. When both trees were planted and matured at Leighton Hall, Montgomeryshire, the new hybrid occurred in 1888. The new bi-generic plant takes part of the generic name from each parent.

Various hybrids may be artificially raised by crossing plants in breeding research programmes. This may be done to produce new and improved varieties.

Curiosity forms have been produced by grafting parts of the plants instead of cross-pollinating flowers. These forms are called graft hybrids and have a new generic name which is preceded with a + sign, e.g.:

+ *Laburnocytisus adamii*
(*Laburnum anagyroides* + *Cytisus purpureus*)

Cultivar

Cultivars are horticulturally selected forms which are cultivated under artificial conditions. For example, trees which have double flowers are not able to produce seed and are, therefore, vegetatively propagated. Most result in exact replicas of the original to become what is termed a 'clone'. Many ornamental and amenity trees are cultivars which have been vegetatively propagated from an abnormality or sport on a wild or cultivated plant. The mature cultivar may produce seed but the resulting seedling will usually revert back to the wild species.

To indicate the status of a cultivar the rules employ two methods:

(a) the abbreviation of cultivar (cv) may be placed before the new third part of the name and the cultivar written with initial capitals, e.g.:

Fraxinus excelsior cv Aurea Pendula (Golden weeping ash)

(b) the cultivar name may be enclosed in single quotation marks and again be written with an initial capital, e.g.:

Fraxinus excelsior 'Pendula' (Weeping ash)

Common names

Common names have the advantage of diversity of use within a language and are popular with the general public. They are obviously simple and pleasing to hear, but as they are not logical or consistent with internationally agreed rules they can lead to confusion. For instance, a single tree may have numerous traditional and folklore names, and this is unsatisfactory for commercial use.

Again, a common name may embrace many different plants in various countries; the common name 'cedar', for example, is used for all the following trees:

Athrotaxis selaginoides "Tasmanian Cedar"
Calocedrus decurrens "Incense Cedar"
Cedrela sinensis "Chinese Cedar"
Cedrus atlantica "Atlas Cedar"
Cryptomeria japonica "Japanese Cedar"
Juniperus virginiana "Pencil Cedar"
Tababuia pallida "White Cedar"
Thuja plicata "Western Red Cedar"

Of these only *Cedrus atlantica* – "Atlas Cedar" – is a true cedar!

Another example of confusion is provided by the mountain ash, which is in fact not an ash (*Fraxinus*) but a *Sorbus*, which means that its alternative name of 'rowan' is the more accurate.

As illustrated above, when the common name is written with the Latin name it is distinguished from the Latin name by being contained in double quotation marks or enclosed in brackets.

3 Tree Growth

P. J. Jordan, MI Biol

When a tree grows its development is influenced by its environment. The requirements of each individual tree will vary depending on its age, vigour, health and situation but it will always have basic needs for light, warmth, air and nutrients. It is important to understand these needs if we are to grow, propagate, plant and maintain our trees in prime condition.

Production of Trees

Seed

Most trees will naturally reproduce themselves by the production of seeds which develop in fruits and cones after the pollination and fertilisation of the flowers. There is a tremendous variety of design in the structure of fruits and seeds which is usually closely linked with the method of seed dispersal which the particular tree has evolved. Many trees and shrubs rely on wind to disperse their seeds and so have developed aerodynamically stable structures like the winged fruits of the ash or the hair-covered seeds of the poplar and willow. Dispersal of seed by animals is also common, species of cherries and plum producing attractive fleshy fruits which are eaten, while the inedible seed is left. Brightly coloured berries containing hard-coated seeds which pass unharmed through the digestive systems of animals are also produced. Many animals will hoard cones and nuts in stores away from the parent tree.

Other methods of dispersal are also employed. The force of gravity itself is important for the distribution of heavy fruits like those of the chestnut and walnut, particularly on steep slopes. Running water is used as the dispersal agent for alder seeds. Whatever system is used, each tree has evolved a method of seed dispersal to carry away the new potential plant so that it does not have to compete with the established parent tree and to limit overcrowding.

Not all of the seeds produced by a tree will grow; many may not be viable. Some species always produce few viable seeds and the percentage produced by old trees is also low. Even if a viable seed is produced and dispersed it still will not germinate unless it is in the right environmental conditions. A supply of oxygen is needed from the air spaces in the soil so that the seed can breathe and release the energy it needs for the embryo to grow. Water is also essential, initially penetrating the seed through the micropyle and then being absorbed through the testa. Once inside the seed the water causes the cells in the seed to become turgid, splitting the testa so that the embryo can grow and dissolving the stored food reserve of the seed so that the solution can be used by the embryo (see fig. 1). All seeds require a reasonable temperature for germination, each species having its own optimum temperature range for ideal germination conditions.

With these environmental requirements – i.e. oxygen, moisture and warmth – satisfied, some seeds will readily germinate, and these species will be commonly propagated by seed in the nursery. However, there are many species of trees which produce seeds which will not germinate immediately in these simple conditions because they are dormant and will require some extra condition to be present before that dormancy can be broken. In nature, seed dormancy has evolved to ensure that germination will start at the right time of year to give the seedling the best chance of survival.

Dormancy can be caused by a number of factors but in tree seeds there are two major causes. Firstly, the seed may have a hard seed coat which prevents oxygen and water from entering in any quantity; it also forms a barrier preventing the embryo from emerging. Secondly, the embryo itself may still be immature even though the seed has fallen from the parent tree. Many tree species produce seeds which have both of these dormancy conditions. The extent of dormancy is difficult to define; in some seeds it is hardly noticeable, being just a slower germination rate, but in others it is shown as a failure to germinate even after two or three years' exposure to suitable conditions. In this case the seed still remains alive but it does not start to grow until the dormancy is broken.

Overcoming seed-coat dormancy is possible artificially either by breaking the testa by cutting or abrading, or by soaking the seed for a short time in water or acid solution. To break dormancy caused by the immaturity of the embryo is more difficult. Seeds with internal embryo dormancy are usually those which are

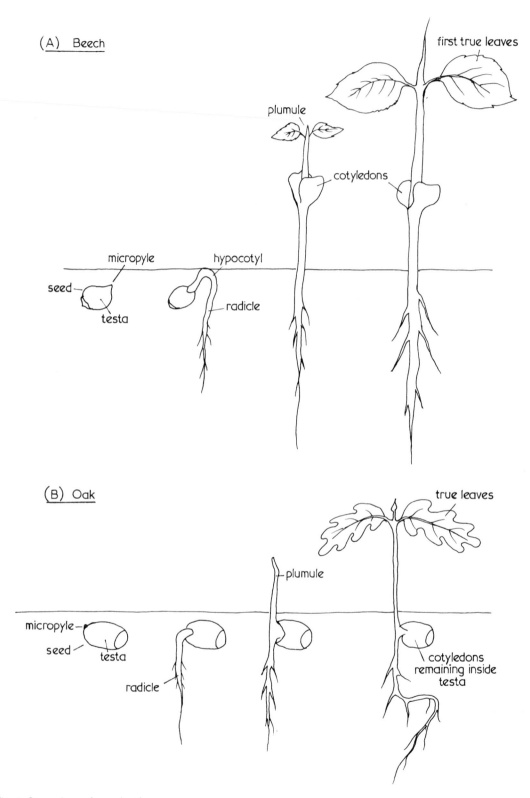

(A) Beech

first true leaves

plumule

cotyledons

micropyle   hypocotyl

seed

testa   radicle

(B) Oak

true leaves

plumule

micropyle

seed   testa

radicle

cotyledons remaining inside testa

Fig. 1 Stages in seed germination

produced by trees in autumn and which in nature would lie on the ground partially covered with litter until the spring before germinating. To break this internal dormancy we have to induce the same changes in the seed as would occur naturally. This is usually achieved by exposing the seed to moisture at low temperatures for some time before sowing.

When a seed starts to germinate water is absorbed through the micropyle and later through the testa itself. The seed is seen to swell as its cells become turgid, the testa splits and the now soluble food reserves are used to produce energy for cell division which causes the seed root or radicle to grow. The radicle emerges into the soil and it begins to take in available water and nutrients. In some seeds part of the radicle elongates to produce a looped hypocotyl which is visible above ground level and as this loop straightens out it pulls the seed's cotyledon food stores and often the testa above ground level (the beech is an example). The cotyledons are the first 'leaves' produced and appear before the seedling shoot or plumule starts to grow (see fig 1A). In other seeds (e.g. oak, chestnut) the cotyledons remain below the ground and the plumule quickly grows and develops its first, true, leaves (see fig 1B).

All seeds, even from the same tree species, do not develop equally well. The origin of the seed is therefore important, since many common tree species like Scots pine, English oak and European beech all produce different races of seed depending on their situaton in varying climatic and soil conditions. Even neighbouring trees of the same species and race still produce seeds and seedlings which vary in structure and vigour, and good seed collection relies on the collector gathering seeds from individual plants or stands which have the most desirable characteristics.

Vegetative propagation

The production of trees from seed is not always practical because the viability of the species may be low, dormancy factors may be difficult to overcome, the vigour of the seedling may be poor or special characteristics may be desired, e.g. a weeping form. In such cases trees can be artifically propagated from their vegetative parts rather than from seed. There are many ways of doing this; the principles are outlined here, and further details may be obtained from Lamb, Kelly and Bowbrick's *Nursery Stock Manual*.

Cuttings
Perhaps the simplest method of vegetative

propagation is to take cuttings from the stem or root. The treatment of a cutting will depend on the maturity of the growth selected and the time of year the cutting is taken. A young green shoot a few weeks old taken in the summer is called a 'soft' cutting. Once taken from the plant the cutting has no means of absorbing water until it has developed its own root system, consequently it will quickly wilt and die. Rooting is often encouraged by using a rooting hormone and keeping the cutting in a shaded, moist, warm atmosphere. Slightly older shoot material can also be used; these cuttings are known as semi-hardwood or half-ripe cuttings, and they also need to be kept in moist shaded conditions until their roots develop. If a fully ripened shoot is taken in the autumn, this is known as a hardwood cutting. About two-thirds of the cutting is buried in open ground where it will normally root and be ready for planting out by the following autumn. Many trees and shrubs, particularly those which sucker freely, can be propagated by inserting small pieces of their roots as cuttings, burying them in well-drained soil. This is best done in the autumn when the foliage has died.

Some species will root easily from cuttings; others will not. The ability to root will depend partly on favourable conditions surrounding the cutting, but also on its internal structure and cell arrangement. For roots to form cell division has to take place within the cutting; most commonly the cambium cells found just below the surface rind or bark of the cutting are responsible for most growth. Externally a mass of quickly produced callus cells are often seen prior to the emergence of the new roots (see fig. 2).

Layering
If a species is difficult to propagate from cuttings or if a large plant is required quickly, layering is another possible method of propagation. The main advantage of this method is that the new plant is not severed from the parent plant until it is self-sufficient and therefore while it is developing it will continue to receive nutrients, food reserves and water from the established parent plant. A suitable branch is selected and pegged into the ground, the flow of sap into the branch being reduced by a cut or twist at the point of entry into the soil. Roots will then form at this point after which the branch can be cut away from the parent plant. Roots will most easily develop from the nodal (joint) areas of bud production on the branch.

Budding and grafting
Budding and grafting are further specialised

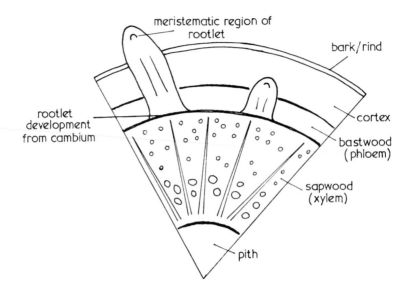

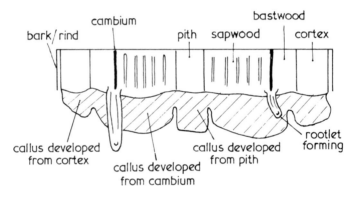

Fig. 2 Transverse and longitudinal sections showing
development of roots from a hardwood cutting

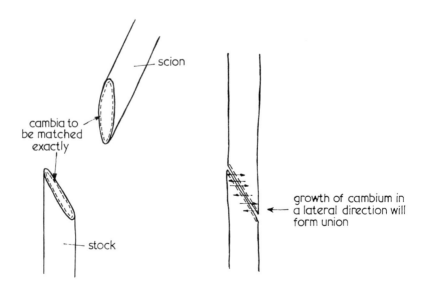

Fig. 3 Cambium growth in a simple whip graft

18

methods of artificial propagation of trees and shrubs. Both involve the combining of the shoot or a shoot bud (scion) of one plant with the rooted portion (stock) of another. This is done to obtain special characteristics in the new plant, e.g. a more vigorous root system with disease resistance, variants in leaf colour, or a change in growth form. Grafting is carried out in late winter or in spring, while budding is a summer operation, and both are skilled techniques. There are many forms of grafting (e.g. wedge, saddle, crown, whip and tongue) and budding (e.g. T budding and, more recently, chip budding) but in all the methods the skill is involved in matching exactly the meristematic cambium cells of the stock and the scion. Cambium cells are capable of dividing only in a horizontal plane and it is essential that with horizontal cambium divison the growing cells should unite the stock and scion to produce a combined cambium area which can go on to develop a permanent union.

Development of Trees

As a seedling grows from a seed, internally its cells differentiate into groups of specialised cells or tissues each of which carry out specific functions. Areas develop which are responsible for water and nutrient (sap) transport through the tree; these are known as xylem areas. Carbohydrates are carried in solution down the tree by phloem areas. Some cells develop thick cell walls and provide strengthening regions for the seedling. Cells capable of dividing (meristematic cells) are also produced, some in the tips of shoots and roots which divide to increase the length and height of the seedling, some – more specialised – dividing only in a lateral direction, so increasing the girth of the seedling. These laterally dividing meristematic cells are cambium and they are responsible for the development of wood.

As the seedling develops in its first season's growth, the cambium cells form a more or less complete ring within the stem and root (see fig. 4A). In the second year the ring starts dividing to make new cells. During this second year and all the subsequent years of the tree's life the ring of cambium cells will divide many times. Each time, any new cells formed inside the cambium ring differentiate into xylem cells and the relatively fewer cells produced on the outside of the cambium ring differentiate into new phloem cells (see fig. 4B).

The cell walls separating each new xylem cell from the one above gradually break down, forming a transporting system of vertical xylem tubes. These tubes become lined with a strengthening material called lignin which gradually builds up over a period of five to ten years until it totally blocks the xylem tubes. The blocked tubes no longer function as living transporting cells but become dead strengthening areas and form the heartwood of the tree. The tree has therefore to rely on the younger living xylem for the circulation of its sap. The young xylem is therefore known as the sapwood. The phloem cells remain as individual units with perforated walls separating each cell from the one above. The phloem areas are known as the bastwood and are responsible, as already indicated, for the circulation of carbohydrate solution down the tree (see fig. 4C).

The rate of cambium division and hence the rate of girth increase depends to a large extent on the environmental conditions affecting the tree. In warm temperatures, when the tree is supplied with a good balance of air and water, cambium division is rapid, and the xylem cells in particular tend to be large and to form an open structure. This would generally occur in spring, and the xylem produced at this time is known as springwood. When the conditions for cambium division deteriorate, as naturally happens in autumn and winter, the xylem cells generally become smaller, forming the denser autumnwood of the tree. The differences in the structure of springwood and autumnwood are clearly seen in trees of temperate climates as annual rings. The development of annual rings in the trunk and branch system is usually very obvious, but in the root system, which is surrounded by soil and has a less varying environment, annual rings are not so clear.

The formation of sapwood and bastwood in the trunk, branch and root areas provides the tree with an efficient up-and-down circulation system, but it is also essential to have some movement of air and solutions across the tree. The medullary or wood rays are developed for this purpose. These are lines of non-lignified cells running across the xylem. Because the ray cells are not strengthened with lignin they tend to be weak points within the wood which will easily split if the tree is damaged.

As the trunk and root system is thickening with age, bark develops to protect the delicate living cells. This is produced from a second specialised cambium known as cork cambium which is formed near the outer edge of the tree. When the cork cambium divides it produces cork cells, the cell walls of which become thickened with two materials: suberin, an oily weatherproofing substance, and tannin, an antiseptic. The bark

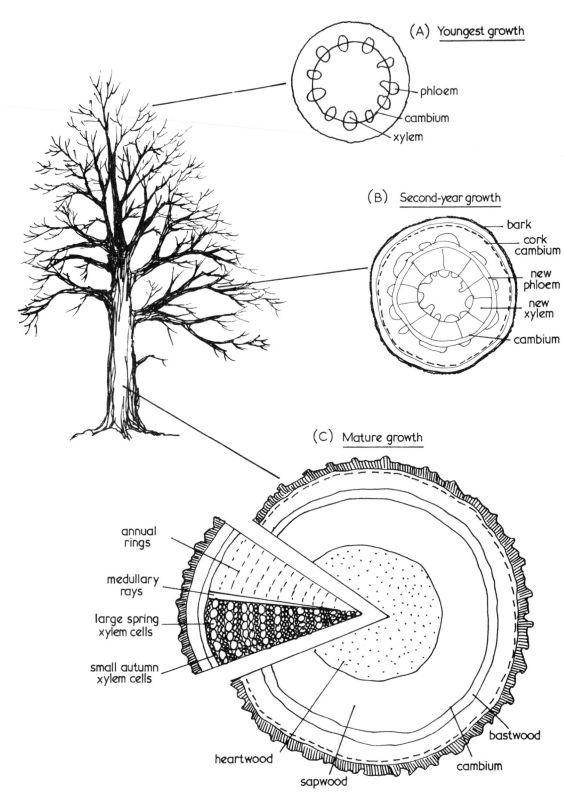

(A) Youngest growth

— phloem

— cambium

— xylem

(B) Second-year growth

— bark
— cork cambium
— new phloem
— new xylem
— cambium

(C) Mature growth

annual rings

medullary rays

large spring xylem cells

small autumn xylem cells

bastwood

heartwood

cambium

sapwood

Fig. 4 The ageing process in the trunk and branches
shown in transverse section

becomes an efficient protective coat acting as an insulator against extreme changes in climate, an antiseptic barrier preventing fungi and bacteria from entering the dead heartwood and decomposing it, and a strong physical barrier protecting the delicate living cells from damage.

The cork cambium itself has only a limited life span of about five years and dead cork cambium is replaced by new living cork cambium developed inside the bastwood. Once a new ring of cork cambium has been made some species of trees (e.g. birch, London plane) will shed their old bark layers leaving a thin smooth new bark. Other species, however (e.g. oak) will keep all the old original bark, developing a thick but deeply fissured rough bark.

Although bark is a very effective protective layer it is not entirely solid and there are weak points within its structure. Some areas of loosely packed cork cells develop into lenticels. Externally these can be seen as small swollen areas which on some species (e.g. flowering cherry) are very obvious. Lenticels are essential in order that gases can be exchanged through the bark from the air to the living cells, and often the position of lenticels is closely linked with the position of the medullary rays in the wood.

All the important living, functioning cells of the tree are therefore situated fairly near to the bark, the bulk of a mature tree being the dead central heartwood. Externally a hollow tree which may be weak and dangerous can appear to be perfectly sound. If an area of bark is ripped or damaged in any way it is most likely that the living bastwood and sapwood and, most important, the cambium will also have been damaged. If a wound is made in a tree the cambium surrounding the damage will try to produce cells to heal it. Since the cambium cells are capable of division only in a horizontal plane, if a wound is made in a vertical direction running along the grain of the wood the cambium cells on either side of the wound can divide relatively easily across the injury, forming a healing callus. However, a relatively small wound encircling the tree is more serious, since the lower cambium cells will have been separated from those above and the cells cannot divide vertically to heal over the gap.

Processes required for Tree Growth

The development of the woody framework of the tree is important as it provides a circulation system for the plant and also gives a strengthened framework on which the leaves, flowers and fruits are supported, but it is not the real working area of the tree. It does not produce or introduce materials into the plant's system enabling it to grow. For the tree to develop as a living organism it needs to have a source of raw materials which can be built up into new cells and hence new growth and it also requires an energy source which can be involved in reactions combining the raw materials together. The parts of the tree important for the drawing in of materials and the production of an energy supply are the roots and the leaves.

Making an energy supply

The leaves are the energy-manufacturing areas without which the tree could not survive. The leaves are able to convert light into a form of chemical energy by the process of photosynthesis. The leaf is designed to produce chemical energy efficiently, initially in the form of carbohydrates. There is no explanation of why such a tremendous variety of leaf shapes and designs should have evolved, but the leaves have certainly achieved a good balance between producing a maximum surface area for the efficient absorption of light for photosynthesis and not developing an excessive area from which the plant would lose water. Even the arrangement of leaves around the twigs is such that each can receive a proportion of the light available.

The chemical reactions involved in photosynthesis are complex and not yet fully understood but the overall result is that pigments concentrated in the top half of the leaf are able to absorb light energy which is used to combine carbon dioxide and water, resulting in the production of carbohydrate and oxygen gas.

$$6\,CO_2 + 6\,H_2O \xrightarrow[\text{by pigments}]{\text{light absorbed}} C_6H_{12}O_6 + 6\,O_2$$

carbon + water dioxide   carbohydrate + oxygen

The major pigment present in most leaves is chlorophyll, a green pigment, though pigments of other colours are also usually present in smaller amounts. Leaves which do not appear to be green will have larger quantities of these other pigments present. Chlorophyll is particularly efficient in absorbing blue and some red wavelengths of light. As light falls on to the surface of the leaf the harmful burning rays are reflected off by the waxy cuticle which allows through the beneficial wavelengths. The light energy passing into the leaf is absorbed by the chlorophyll and this energy is used to initiate a

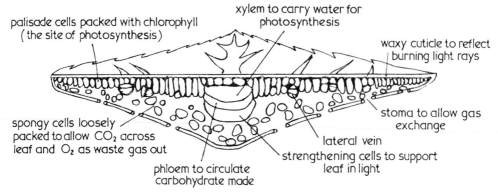

palisade cells packed with chlorophyll
(the site of photosynthesis)

xylem to carry water for
photosynthesis

waxy cuticle to reflect
burning light rays

spongy cells loosely
packed to allow CO_2 across
leaf and O_2 as waste gas out

stoma to allow gas
exchange

lateral vein

strengthening cells to support
leaf in light

phloem to circulate
carbohydrate made

Fig. 5 Leaf structure and photosynthesis

complex series of reactions to combine water originally supplied from the soil via the xylem system and carbon dioxide coming from the air through stomatal pores on the leaf. The result is that carbohydrate is produced which is circulated to every living cell in the tree through its phloem system. The oxygen by-product is expelled into the air through the stomatal pores.

Many factors will control the rate of photosynthesis and consequently the amount of carbohydrate produced. The area of each leaf's light-receiving surface and the chlorophyll concentration is important, and deciduous trees obviously do not photosynthesise in winter. The age of the leaves also has an effect, younger leaves being the most efficient at absorbing light. The amount of light available with varying numbers of daylight hours is significant, as is the intensity of the light received, which changes with the seasons and may be reduced by pollution or shading. The water available to the tree is often a limiting factor, being essential not only as a starting agent for the reaction but also to maintain the turgidity of the leaves and to keep the stomatal pores open. Photosynthesis is also influenced by temperature, the reaction not occurring below $4\,°C$, so that even evergreen trees may not be photosynthesising in winter. With an increase in temperature of the rate of the reaction will speed up until the point is reached at which scorch damage occurs. The concentration of carbon dioxide in the air is rarely a limiting factor of photosynthetic rate in natural conditions.

Releasing energy for use
Once the carbohydrate produced in photosynthesis has been circulated to supply all the tree's living cells, any excess is often stored in the root system or in fruits and seeds. Carbohydrate itself is not a directly usable energy source. In order to release usable energy from it each plant cell has to respire. For respiration or breathing each cell must normally be supplied with oxygen.

$$C_6H_{12}O_6 + 6\,O_2 \xrightarrow{\text{Energy Released}} 6\,H_2O + 6\,CO_2$$

carbohydrate + oxygen → water + carbon dioxide

Supplying oxygen to the outer aerial parts of the tree is simple since they are surrounded by air, but an air supply to the internal cells is more difficult. Lenticels and stomata are used to allow air into the tree and it then diffuses through a network of spaces found between the plant's cells. The root cells have to obtain their oxygen from the air spaces in the soil and thus the root system is the part of the tree most commonly starved of an adequate oxygen supply. In soils which are compacted, waterlogged or polluted there is little air available for the roots. Trees can survive temporarily in airless soils by respiring anaerobically. This will release some energy from carbohydrate, but not sufficient to sustain good healthy growth. Furthermore, alcohol is built up as a waste product of anaerobic respiration, and this is toxic, killing the root cells. Trees which grow naturally in wet soils, like willows and poplars, tend to develop shallow root systems extending through the soil above the level of the water table where air is still present. Trees which find themselves in prolonged flooded conditions soon begin to show signs of ill-health as the root system becomes inefficient and starts to rot away.

Taking in water and nutrients
As well as requiring an energy source for survival, trees also need to obtain water and nutrients from the soil. The root system is obviously the area concerned with uptake from the soil, the materials then being transported to all parts of the tree by means of the xylem system. Tree root systems tend to be very extensive. Many self-sown trees will develop one major deep root

(known as the tap root) which gives the tree good anchorage, plus a mass of finer wide-spreading feeding roots nearer to the soil surface. Some trees, however, do not have a tap root – beech, notorious for its instability, has only a very shallow root system – and trees which have been transplanted will have had their tap roots undercut in the nursery or when lifted. Once the tap root has been cut it will not grow again, but the tree reacts by producing additional fine fibrous roots in the topsoil where water and nutrients tend to be more readily available.

It is only the root hairs on the young growth at the tip of each root which are concerned with uptake from the soil. In the harsh abrasive environment of the soil these root hairs gradually get worn away and on the older root growth they are replaced by ordinary protective cells rather than by new root hairs. Each root hair is only a single cell which has an elongated shape and therefore a large surface area in contact with the soil solution held between the soil particles. As long as the soil solution is less concentrated than the sap in the root hair, water will be drawn into the root hair by osmosis. In some situations the soil solution may become too concentrated – a drought, for example, reduces the water content of the soil, or pollution may be present. In such conditions the soil solution becomes more concentrated than the root-hair sap, so that water is drawn out of the plant. This leads to permanent damage of the root-hair structure, known as plasmolysis, and the root hair cannot take up any soil materials. Plasmolysis also occurs if a concentration of fertiliser comes into contact with the root hairs. It is therefore particularly important not to allow fertilisers to touch bare roots if they are being used when a tree is planted. The damage occurs rapidly, with the root hair being killed within a few minutes of fertiliser contact. Root hairs are very delicate and easily damaged and it is important to always treat them carefully, preventing them from drying out and losing their turgidity.

The root hairs are also responsible for the uptake of minerals or nutrients from the soil. All trees require a range of nutrients including nitrogen, phosphorus and potassium in large quantities, sulphur, magnesium, calcium and iron in smaller amounts and copper, zinc, molybdenum, manganese and boron in minute quantities. All of these nutrients are equally important and if any one is missing the tree will develop a deficiency symptom. The root hairs are selective to some degree, allowing only certain elements to enter, but they have little control over the quantity of each nutrient taken in. If a particular nutrient is freely available in the soil solution it will flow into the root hair down the existing concentration gradient, and it is thus possible for toxic quantities of a nutrient to flow in; hence the importance of maintaining a balanced soil-nutrient status.

Normally many of the nutrients required by the tree will not be present in large enough quantities to be freely available, and the tree has actively to draw in these nutrients, using energy to pull them in against the concentration gradient. The availability of nutrients is determined not only by their presence or absence in the soil but also by their solubility. Minerals become more soluble and hence more available as the soil temperature rises. The soil pH (acidity or alkalinity level) will also determine whether nutrients will dissolve. At a neutral pH of about 6·5–7·0 all the major plant nutrients are soluble and therefore available for uptake. As the soil solution becomes more acidic or alkaline some minerals will not dissolve easily and are therefore difficult for the tree to take in. Trees which naturally grow in acidic conditions (e.g. pines) or in alkaline soils (e.g. beech) have developed symbiotic associations with mycorrhizal fungi which pass to the tree nutrients which otherwise would be unavailable. In return for the nutrients the tree supplies the fungi with carbohydrate.

Sap flow
Once inside the root system the water and nutrient solution becomes the sap and is circulated to all parts of the tree by way of the living xylem cells. The pressure required to lift the sap up the height of the tree against the force of gravity is enormous and this lift in sap is largely achieved by a suction exerted from the leaves known as transpiration pull. Large quantities of water are lost in transpiration by evaporation through the stomata on the leaves; on a hot summer's day hundreds of litres of water can be lost by a mature tree. This loss of water sets up a suction force which draws the sap up the xylem tubes as a continuous stream. The stomatal pores are able to open and close, which operation is indirectly controlled by photosynthesis; generally the pores will be open during the day, releasing water, and closed at night, retaining water. The stomatal pores will only stay open if the guard cells surrounding them are turgid; if the turgidity is lost because the tree is short of water the pores quickly close, thus providing a good emergency mechanism to prevent excessive transpiration.

All of the water lost by transpiration has to be replaced by the tree's root system from the soil. If the root system is not efficient enough to do this, wilting and eventually death will occur. Trees which grow naturally in dry soils or exposed conditions have evolved structurally to minimise transpiration by developing, for example, thick cuticles or small leaf-surface areas, as in conifers.

Conclusion

All plants have to be considered as entire living organisms. Although the roots, leaves, branches and flowers have their individual functions, the performance of each will affect the efficiency of the others. If any part of the tree is damaged it is bound to have an effect on the remainder of the plant's system. Transplanting trees may at first glance affect only the root system, but this influences nutrient uptake and hence growth, water uptake and turgidity, controlling stomatal opening and consequently photosynthesis, respiration and transpiration. Crown thinning may appear to affect only the crown, but this in turn reduces transpiration and sap circulation; it reduces photosynthesis and therefore the energy reserves available for use and storage in fruits and seeds. All parts of the tree are therefore interdependent.

4 Selection of Trees

The selection of the right tree to suit the planting conditions and situation is one of the chief prerequisites for successful establishment. We see far too many examples of faulty selection resulting in trees failing to grow or being out of scale with their surroundings and often creating problems and the need for expensive pruning or felling.

There is such a vast range of species available that it is always possible to select a tree or group of trees that will provide the desired characteristics and not cause problems. Whether selecting a single tree for a front garden or several thousands for large-scale schemes it is important to consider the following factors which will influence your choice:

1 Characteristics desired
2 Ultimate size and shape
3 Soil type and condition
4 Environmental conditions
5 Size and type of transplant
6 Availability and purchasing

1 Characteristics Desired

Trees, by their longevity and range of shapes, sizes and colours, provide the backbone of our landscape in both town and country. They are often just taken for granted, but in most places they were once planted by someone, and they are not indestructible.

Individual trees for gardens

For town garden planting it is good to see individual preferences expressed, and many towns and housing estates are richly enhanced by the wide range of trees. Some people will prefer the smaller-growing trees and spring-flowering species; others like autumn leaf colour or fruit. Careful selection could offer both. Where a screen is required for privacy or shelter, then evergreens, particularly conifers, can be planted.

Nurserymen's catalogues and books with colour illustrations will help guide the householder. A visit to the local garden centre will show what is available, and advice can be sought on the size and characteristics of the trees and their suitability to local conditions. (Appendix 2, the Tree Directory, suggests trees of various attractions and forms.)

Group planting schemes

Where a group of trees is to be planted, thought should be given to the long-term effect. In towns a wide range of sizes and forms can be selected to give attractive features throughout the season. Where there is space the larger-growing types can be planted, with small or medium-sized trees in confined situations. Try to avoid repetition, and consider bold groups of trees planted closely together rather than straight lines of one type – unless in a formal avenue.

1 A small upright-growing flowering pear tree for planting in a confined space between buildings

2 Birch trees requiring more space but suitable for both town gardens and country planting

3 Large-growing Robinia and maples planted in a grass area with room to grow to their full proportions. Note 'Weldmesh' tree guards (see p. 50) protecting trunks

Planting in the countryside

Where it is planned to plant trees in country areas, preference should be given to those types which will harmonise with the natural trees already growing in the locality. The limited range of 'native' trees will often suit the majority of the sites but other naturalised trees such as the sweet and horse chestnut, walnut, Turkey oak, sycamore and Norway maple will give variety and will look in keeping with the rural scene. Avoid the ornamental cherries and vivid-coloured trees, which are best planted in town gardens.

Local Authority planting

The local county, borough or district council will be responsibile for trees in streets, parks, housing estates, schools, etc., and will often employ professionally qualified staff. Their policies should ensure a good range of species to avoid repetition and the risk of epidemic disease affecting one particular species or family of trees.

In the past many councils did not have professional staff, and some still do not. We see the problems of towns which have inherited expensive maintenance problems with large trees in small streets, and others with a high proportion of one species, such as elm. The threat

4 Planting and retention of oaks in the countryside

Picea abies

to their tree population is now enormous, and they could be faced not only with the complete loss of their trees but also with a very large bill for felling. As a guide, the overall tree selection policy of a local authority should ensure that no more than 10 per cent of the planting is of any one genus, and no more than 20 per cent of any one family.

2 Ultimate Size and Shape of Trees and Roots

Thought must always be given to the mature height and spread of the tree and its roots.

Where there is space, e.g. on village greens or in large gardens or the countryside, the larger-growing trees will ultimately provide the best amenity.

Trees planted close to structures should be in scale with the buildings. London plane trees are well suited to the squares and parks of our cities but could completely overshadow a small bungalow. One of the most common mistakes is to plant a weeping willow in a small front or rear garden. Within fifteen years it could be creating problems by the spread of its branches and roots.

Trees should have sufficient room to grow to their natural proportions without the need for unsightly and expensive pruning. On the other hand, they should not be too small: a small flowering crab apple would never provide any real lasting amenity in a large open space. (The Tree Directory gives the sizes of some of the most commonly planted trees.)

When positioning trees, look out for overhead power cables and telephone lines and site the trees so as not to create too much shade on the neighbouring property.

It is important to consider the spread of the roots. Basically, the larger the tree the greater the spread of the roots. An old rule of thumb suggests that the tree's roots spread approximately as far as its branches. It was assumed that most of the roots developed around the drip line, or where the majority of the rain fell. This may be so for some species, but it has been found that the roots of many larger-growing trees can spread considerably further, although they rarely go deeper than about 1m (3–4ft).

Tree roots can cause real difficulties in lawns and gardens, and one of the greatest problems is where large trees are planted close to buildings on shrinkable clay soils. Since the 1976 drought conditions there have been many examples of actual damage caused by the shrinkage and settlement of the clay soil, and in some cases tree

28

5 Feathered alders for natural-looking countryside
  planting

6 Large-growing ash trees planted in a narrow street
  and thus requiring regular expensive and ugly
  pruning to control their size

7 A common mistake: planting large-growing
weeping willows too close to houses

roots will contribute to this problem by removing soil water. When selecting trees for planting close to buildings on shrinkable clay it is best to avoid vigorous trees such as poplars and willows; and, unless the buildings have deep foundations, do not plant within a distance equal to one and a half times the ultimate height of any large-growing tree.

3 Soil Type and Condition

Most trees will grow in a range of soil types and conditions and only the extremes of the range – e.g. very wet or dry soils, extremely acid conditions, or reclaimed industrial waste – will limit the selection.

Some individual tree species, however, are more choosy and will only establish and grow successfully if the planting conditions are correct. To try to change or improve the soil conditions to suit these species can be very expensive, and it is often better to select more tolerant types. As a guide, look to see which species are growing successfully in your locality, and this will help selection. (The Tree Directory suggests suitable species for some of the various soil conditions found in the UK.)

On housing sites the soil has often been disturbed, with only a covering of topsoil being left over brick rubble and builders' debris. In such cases some soil improvements will be necessary to give the tree a chance to establish. (See Chapter 5, Tree Planting.)

4 Environmental Conditions

Apart from soil conditions, it is also important to consider any other factors that will limit the choice of trees, e.g. climate, seaside conditions, pollution, vandalism, and pests and diseases.

Climate

Being a comparatively small group of islands, the UK has a very variable climate, and the influences of the main continent and the Atlantic Ocean result in widely differing conditions in various parts of the country. The south-west, for example, is comparatively mild, as are parts of western Scotland, and even some half-hardy trees can be successfully grown there. In the northern parts of Scotland and on the east coast, on the other hand, the conditions are often very harsh and cold, resulting in stunted growth of even the tough hardy trees. The average rainfall in parts of the west coast can be four or five times that of south-east England. The UK is also very prone to high winds, and in exposed areas only certain species will establish, particularly at altitude and by the coast.

Trees in groups or woodlands can create their own microclimate and provide their own shelter, shade and protection. Town centres can be several degrees warmer in the winter than the open country, but tall buildings can increase wind speed and alter wind direction, creating very draughty and unpleasant conditions.

The fact that much of the rainwater in towns is lost through drainage into the sewerage system can result in very dry garden soils.

All of these variable climatic factors will influence the choice of trees. (The Tree Directory lists trees suitable for some of the extremes of our climate.)

Seaside conditions
Many parts of the mainland of the UK and all of the smaller islands are influenced by the sea. Generally, coastal conditions are exposed and windy, and many trees will be damaged or shaped by salt-laden winds. Establishing even 'tough' species in such sites can be difficult and often some form of shelter will need to be provided.

However, southern and western coastal areas are often milder in winter than inland areas, and some trees which are frost-tender will tolerate exposed seaside conditions. (The Tree Directory suggests trees for exposed seaside conditions.)

Pollution
The clean air regulations have greatly reduced the air pollution problems in our towns and cities, but many industrial areas can create unsuitable conditions and affect tree growth. Evergreens and conifers are worst affected because their leaves remain on the trees for longer periods and become blocked with dust and grime. It is not possible to clean the leaves, therefore it is best to select deciduous types in the worst-affected areas.

The application of road salt in the winter can again produce very hostile conditions, with the spray from fast-moving vehicles creating almost seaside conditions. Highway authorities should ensure that salt storage heaps are located well clear of trees in order to avoid pollution of the soil.

8 Vandalism on trees close to an unofficial footpath

Vandalism

It is not the objective of this book to solve the social problems which cause the wilful destruction of our environment, but this factor must be considered when selecting the type and size of tree to be planted. The use of larger-sized transplants which are not so easily pulled up, and the planting of thorned or prickly trees or surrounding shrubs, can help reduce the likelihood of damage.

Involving children in tree-planting schemes and using trees and woodlands for nature study can help to create an understanding of the importance of trees in our landscape and thus to prevent vandalism.

Pests and diseases

The presence of pests or diseases on a site may again influence the choice of trees. Many soil-borne pests or diseases will attack newly planted trees, or insects or disease spores may spread from neighbouring trees. (See Chapter 12, Tree Disorders.)

5 Size and Type of Transplant

Basically, the smaller and younger the transplants the greater the chance of successful establishment and the lower the cost. However, because of the various constraints and problems

9   Trees growing successfully only 20m (65ft) from those shown in pl. 8. The thorned shrubs prevent access

10   Encouraging children's interest in trees can help prevent vandalism in the long term

11   Large-scale forestry production of trees from seed

encountered in the planting area it is often necessary to plant quite large trees. It is, therefore, essential to consider carefully the various sizes and types available and to select the most suitable.

Although there is some variation in practice and descriptions from one nursery to another, transplants can be divided into four main size categories:

1 Forest transplants and whips
2 Nursery stock trees
3 Advanced nursery stock trees
4 Semi-mature trees

1 Forest transplants and whips
The cheapest and smallest of transplant sizes. Used for large-scale plantations, screen planting, land reclamation, soil stabilisation and hedging, and as root stocks for the more ornamental varieties.

Because they are small, they require comparatively little soil preparation or improvement, are quickly and easily planted and should not require staking. As they are planted on a large scale, maintenance will be difficult, but except in very dry summers they should be able to fend for themselves. However, they can easily be suppressed by weed growth, so a clear area should be maintained around each tree. (See Maintenance of Transplants, p. 54.)

Can be purchased as a seedling, a transplant or a whip.

Seedlings
Lifted from seed-beds and sold direct at either one or two years old, and up to 1m (approx 3ft) high. Should have a single strong stem and good fibrous roots. Can be undercut in the seedbeds to induce fibrous roots.

Transplants
Seedlings lifted and lined out and grown on for a further one or two years up to 1m (approx 3ft) high. Some species require this additional time in the nursery to produce a tree which will withstand the planting-site conditions. Should have single strong stem and good fibrous root system.

Whips
This category includes transplants and trees grown from cuttings, budding or grafting. Price and size will vary according to the method of production. Sizes from 1 to 2·5m (3–8ft) without significant branches. The larger whips may require supporting.

2 Nursery stock trees
Trees grown on from the smaller categories to sizes between 1·8 and 3·5m (6ft–11ft 6in).

All are transplanted in the nursery to produce a fibrous root system. They are normally lifted without any soil (bare root) and will require a specially prepared tree pit, good planting soil and staking. Being larger than the first category they will have more immediate visual effect, but are still small enough to be easily broken by vandals.

They can be purchased with branches to ground level (feathered) or with a clear stem (standard).

Feathered trees
Should have a strong central leader with evenly balanced branches near to or at ground level. Very effective for screen and shelter planting, for

Fig. 6 Feathered tree

game and wildlife cover and for countryside planting. It is possible to obtain multi-stemmed feathered trees and these can be effectively planted in groups to give low natural-looking cover.

Standard trees
Probably the size most commonly planted in amenity tree-planting schemes. Differs from the feathered tree in having the lower branches removed to give a clear stem to a specified height (see fig 7). Suitable for gardens, parks and street tree planting.

3 Advanced nursery stock trees
Nursery stock trees grown on for a further few years to produce a larger transplant between 3·6 and 6m (12–20ft) high. Some of the more easily

12 Production of advanced nursery stock trees in a 'tree bank'

13 Advanced nursery stock trees and standards
providing amenity in a shopping precinct

transplanted trees can still be lifted with bare roots but the majority will require a root ball. This root ball not only reduces root disturbance but if kept firm and intact during transit can help anchor the tree at the final planting site. These larger trees will normally require some mechanical aids for lifting and transporting but can still be manhandled into the planting hole.

This size of tree is particularly useful where an immediate visual effect is required or where there is a high risk of vandalism of the smaller types.

Although expensive compared with the smaller categories, these trees can be cost-effective and the expenditure is justified on large-scale housing sites, in shopping precincts, etc.

4 Semi-mature trees
Very large transplants up to 9m (30ft) high. Although they are very expensive, the outlay can occasionally be justified on very prestigious sites. Semi-mature trees require a large root ball and

specialist lifting machinery, and normally need guying and very thorough maintenance.

Root systems

Bare root
The smaller transplants can be lifted and planted without any soil. There should be an abundance of small fibrous roots spaced evenly around the stem. Ensure that the roots are kept moist and protected from sun, wind and frost.

Root-wrapped
Most ornamental conifers and some of the more difficult species should be lifted with a soil ball and immediately wrapped in hessian or netting. This soil ball helps protect the roots and retains moisture. Ensure that the soil remains moist if there is any delay between lifting and planting, and handle the tree carefully to prevent the ball of soil collapsing.

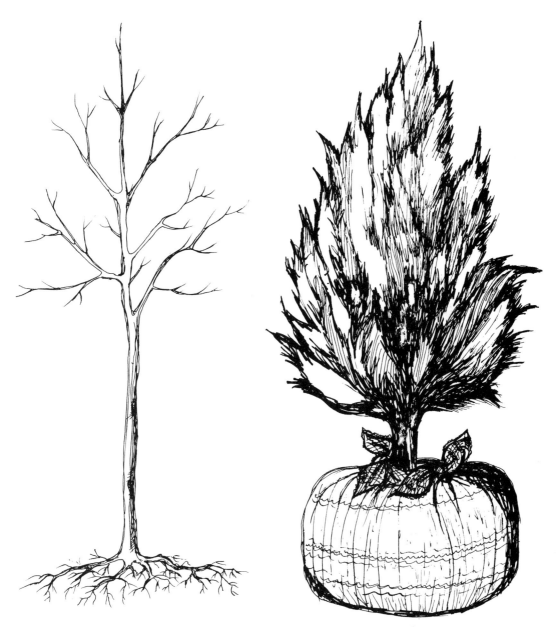

Fig. 7 Standard bare-root tree

Fig. 8 Root-wrapped conifer

Root-balled

The larger categories of transplants will require a solid root ball. The root ball should contain the majority of the roots; this can be achieved by transplanting the trees regularly in the nursery or, with the semi-mature trees, by careful preparation a year or two in advance of lifting (see p. 51). The root ball should be wrapped in hessian or canvas and tying-in with rope may be required to help prevent the ball collapsing.

Container-grown trees

Many garden centres will be able to supply whips and nursery stock trees grown in pots. This means that there is no root damage as there is when the trees are lifted from the nursery, and that trees can be planted outside the normal planting seasons. The extra cost of the container, compost and labour will result in a more expensive tree, but this may be worthwhile if planting needs to be carried out in the late spring or summer. Also the heavy root ball can reduce the need for staking.

There is a risk that a tree may be left in the container far too long and the roots may girdle the pot. With large-growing types this could be

Fig. 9 Root-balled tree

14 Container-grown large trees suitable for lifting and planting virtually all the year round, as the roots are not disturbed

potentially dangerous as these girdling roots could, in the long term, strangle the tree and cause it to fall.

Many advanced nursery stock trees are also grown in containers.

6 Availability and Purchasing

After deciding on the attractions, tolerances and sizes of trees, it is necessary to see which are available through the nursery trade and to compare prices. Trees grown from seed are cheaper to produce than those requiring expensive facilities and labour, such as the grafted types. Some nurseries produce large

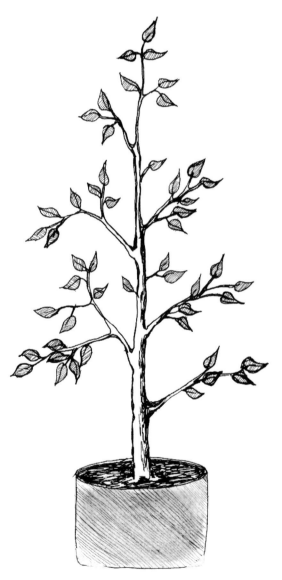

Fig. 10 Container-grown tree

quantities of a limited range of species to enable mechanisation to reduce labour costs. Others specialise in the more difficult and expensive forms. Trees sold with bare roots will be cheaper than those which require root-wrapping, balling or containers. These factors must be considered carefully as limited funds may well govern the selection.

Most nurseries produce annual catalogues which list species, types and sizes available, together with the prices. For small-scale planting schemes individuals or groups can usually find suitable trees at a local garden centre. There you can see what is offered and seek guidance on the tree's suitability for your area. For larger-scale schemes it is advisable to prepare a list of species and sizes and invite quotations from the various nurseries. Remember that catalogue prices may be subject to delivery charges and VAT.

A model specification for the supply and delivery of nursery stock trees is produced by the Joint Council for Landscape Industries (JCLI). An annual plant list which gives the range of trees and shrubs available from the British nursery sector is produced by the Horticultural Trades Association (HTA).

If buying by mail order you do not have the benefit of seeing the plants in advance, so always inspect the trees carefully on delivery and reject any that do not come up to standard.

Whatever the source, always check for the following points:

1 Trees should be true to name (not substitutes).
2 Larger-growing types should have a clear central leader and well-balanced branch system.
3 Bushy types should have a well-balanced crown.
4 All trees should have a strong stem with a minimum diameter related to the height of the tree.
5 Bare-root trees should have sufficient roots to support the tree and there should be ample fine (fibrous) roots.
6 Root-wrapped or root-balled trees should have a secure, firm, moist root ball.
7 Container-grown trees should not have any large roots girdling the container.
8 All trees should be free of major damage to roots, stem or branches.
9 There should be no weeds on the roots or in the soil ball.
10 There should be no signs of pests or diseases.

Detailed specifications for tree transplants are available in British Standards (see p. 118).

5 Tree Planting

To give continuity to our landscape and to replace trees lost through disease, drought and development we must plant more and more. Tree planting follows the same principles as for any plant form. Once we have selected our tree we must determine the actual planting position, plant at the correct time of the year, prepare the soil thoroughly, plant at the right depth and firmness, and adequately support and maintain the tree until established.

Planting Sites

Most people will have sufficient space in their garden to plant at least one small tree. Those with larger gardens or estates and those responsible for trees in a parish or town can find many sites where trees can be planted to good effect. Even flat-dwellers can become involved by helping others to plant on village greens, on spare ground in towns or in the countryside.

If planting on your own land, find a suitable site so that the trees, as they mature, will not cause a nuisance. Be careful not to plant under overhead power or telephone cables, position to give maximum effect and screening and ensure that there is sufficient space for the tree to grow to its full proportions without expensive and unsightly lopping.

If planning to plant on land owned by others, always seek their permission and check who will pay for the planting and future maintenance.

The ravages of disease, drought, fire, new roads and buildings and hedgerow clearance have created many treeless areas and there should be no difficulty in finding suitable sites. The local parish or district council may also be able to suggest planting areas. If planting on or near roads ensure that you comply with the highway regulations (see Chapter 11, Legal Responsibilities).

Seasons for Planting

The normal planting time for deciduous trees is the dormant season, i.e. from leaf-fall in autumn to leaf-break in spring. However, it is preferable to plant as early as possible in November and to complete the planting before Christmas. During these two months the soil should still be in good condition and the tree will have a chance to settle in before the period of spring growth. Trees that bleed profusely when cut in the early spring (e.g. birch and maples) should be planted before Christmas.

Planting *can* be carried out during January, February and March, but ensure that the soil is in good condition, i.e. not frozen or too wet.

For evergreen trees, particularly conifers, it is best to plant in the spring (April/May). As the leaves are still present to lose water, the trees could suffer during the winter before the roots can grow in the spring.

If the trees are grown in containers it is possible to plant outside these normal seasons as the roots should not be unduly disturbed. However, avoid planting during very dry spells in the summer.

There are means of extending the planting season. Anti-transpirant sprays are available which can be applied to the leaves to reduce water loss. If applied thoroughly, such a spray enables deciduous trees to be planted after leaf-break and will help evergreen trees at any season of the year.

For large-scale planting of small transplants, it is possible to keep the trees dormant by placing them in cold storage. They can then be planted in May/June when the conditions will be more suitable, particularly in upland and northern areas.

Soil Preparation

It will be necessary to carry out some soil preparation for all categories of transplants. Basically, the smaller the tree and the better the existing soil, the less preparation will be required. It is better to select trees tolerant of the existing soil than to try to change the soil conditions. If it is necessary to improve the soil (e.g. by drainage), this should be carried out before planting.

Small transplants and whips will require only the minimum of soil preparation. On good deep loamy soils it will only be necessary to excavate a hole as large as the root spread and to replace the same soil over the roots. If the soil is poor or shallow it will be necessary to provide some soil-improvement materials. A hole is excavated at least as large as the root spread, the poor soil is

15 Planting a standard nursery stock tree:
preparation of a suitably sized hole, forking over
the base, incorporating organic material and re-
firming

removed and the tree then planted in good
imported soil.

Feathered and standard nursery stock trees will
require a larger tree pit. Ensure that the
excavated hole is at least 150mm (6in) greater in
radius than the root spread. On average the tree
pit will be approximately 1m×1m×300mm deep
(3ft×3ft×1ft). If good, the existing soil can be
used for planting; if poor, it is advisable to replace
it or improve it with bulky organic materials
(humus). On heavy or compacted soils, fork over
the base of the hole and again add humus. If the
sides of the tree pit appear glazed (clay soil),
break up this surface by forking to allow root
penetration.

Advanced nursery stock trees will require a tree pit
at least 300mm (1ft) greater in radius and
150mm (6in) deeper than the root ball. As before,
fork over the base of the pit and replace or
improve the back-fill soil.

Semi-mature trees will require a pit at least
600mm (2ft) greater in radius and 300mm (1ft)
deeper than the root ball.

Soil improvement materials
Bulky organic material (humus) incorporated
into the base of the pit and/or into the back-fill
soil will greatly improve the transplant's chances
of survival. It will help drainage on heavy soils
and retain moisture on sandy or gravelly soil, and
some types will supply plant foods.

41

Peat is often used as it performs all the necessary functions apart from supplying plant food; fertiliser can be added to correct this deficiency.

Natural leaf-mould collected from woodlands or decomposed after leaf-fall is a very good material. However, ensure that it is well decomposed and free from harmful pests and diseases.

Farmyard manure has been used, but this can contain harmful diseases such as Phytophthora and should not in any case come into direct contact with the bare roots.

Garden compost is very useful for garden planting. Again ensure that it is well decomposed and free of weeds.

Proprietary planting composts are available through garden centres and nurseries. These are, by comparison, expensive but do contain the humus and nutrients necessary for successful establishment.

Fertiliser can be used to supply the necessary plant foods, being mixed into the planting soil or peat. It is preferable to use a slow-release compound granular type as this will supply the nutrients over several months. Strong fertilisers must not be allowed to come into direct contact with the roots.

For small-scale planting schemes the trees pits can be excavated by hand using a spade and fork. On housing estates and on shallow soils a pickaxe may be required.

For larger schemes it is worth considering employing mechanical aids. A digger attachment on a tractor will soon excavate the hole so long as there is access for the machine. Soil auger attachments are also available and can drill out a hole up to 600mm (2ft) in diameter.

Do not prepare the tree pits too far in advance of planting as they will fill with water in wet weather or may be filled in, trampled on or fallen into by children.

If the base of the planting hole has been forked over, re-firm by treading with the feet to avoid undue settlement. If planting in a lawn, first remove the turf. This can be used elsewhere or broken up and placed at the base of the hole.

Make sure the planting soil is friable (fine-textured) so that it can be evenly spread over the fine roots.

Planting tools and equipment

For trees up to the nursery stock size, conventional gardening hand tools are all that is required for tree planting. A spade and fork will be needed for excavating the tree pit and for planting. If the soil is very hard and compacted, or if there is a solid subsoil, a pickaxe or mattock may be necessary.

When stakes are to be used, these should be driven into the ground with a large sledge-hammer or wooden mallet. Steps will be required and a second person should be on hand to steady the steps and hold the stake upright while it is driven in. On larger planting schemes a post-driver will be more efficient. Although these perform the operation more quickly, without the need for steps, they are very heavy and should be used with care (see pl. 20).

Stakes should be large enough to penetrate the undisturbed soil beneath the tree pit and extend high enough into the crown of the tree to give support. The larger categories of transplants may well require more than one stake, or guying (see p. 53). If planting on a site where vandalism is likely, it is better to use longer stakes that will be higher in the crown to prevent vandals breaking off the tree at the top of the stake. Round or cleft stakes are preferable to the sawn types, as they should be straight-grained.

If the stakes are of timber other than sweet chestnut or larch they should be treated with a wood preservative. The best types are those which have been pressure-treated with preservative; these will last for several years without rotting. The stakes should be pointed at the thicker end and should have their bark removed.

Tree ties for securing the tree to the stake are available through nurseries and garden centres. String or wire should not be used as it will quickly damage the stem of the tree.

A range of proprietary brands is available. The buckle type are ideal as they are easily fixed and adjusted and give firm support (see pl. 24). The nail-on type should be used where there is a risk of vandalism.

Ensure that the ties are fixed securely to prevent the tree rubbing on the stake.

Guards to protect the trunk from animals or vandals are available in a range of types and sizes. These should be fixed to give maximum protection, but not in such a position that they can damage the tree. In busy pedestrian areas the 'Weldmesh' type can act as a litter bin; therefore, leave a small space at the bottom to allow for the removal of any debris. (See pls. 3, 16–19.)

Grilles may be required if planting in pavements or shopping precincts. These are available in iron or concrete and their function is to give access around the tree without undue compaction. They should not be in a position to damage the trunk and must allow water penetration (see pls. 27–9).

Mulching (applying a layer of organic or inorganic material over the soil after planting) is

16 A 'Rainbow' plastic rabbit guard   17 'Netlon' rabbit guard

18 Iron cattle guard: very effective and durable, but often costs more than the tree

19 Wooden tree stakes and fencing wire providing a cheap temporary cattle guard

very valuable as it helps to retain moisture, suppresses weed growth, keeps the temperature more even and can supply nutrients.

The soil improvement materials listed on pp. 41–2 are ideal for the tree, but they are bulky and can be messy. Inorganic materials such as gravel help to retain moisture but supply no nutrients and in pedestrian areas are easily thrown or scattered.

An artificial mulch material called a 'Treespat' is also available. This has the qualities of bulky types but is easy to carry and fix and is degradable over about five years (see pl. 26).

Planting and Supporting Trees

When trees are first received from the nursery it is important to give them adequate protection until planting. As there is often a few days' delay between delivery and planting, the small delicate fibrous roots on bare-root trees will easily be destroyed by strong sun, drying winds or frost. Therefore, the tree should be 'heeled in' or temporarily planted. Ensure that the roots are covered by soil, leaf-mould or straw. If the delay is only for a few hours simply cover the roots with sacking.

Check the tree before planting and remove any broken branches or roots. Use a clean pair of secateurs and cut off beyond the damaged area; it is advisable to paint the cuts with a tree paint.

The method of planting and supporting the tree will depend on the size of the transplant and whether it has bare roots or root-wrapping or is root-balled.

Bare-root trees
Small transplants and whips will not normally require supports but larger feathered and standard trees almost certainly will, particularly if planted in exposed positions.

To avoid damaging the roots it is necessary to drive in the stake first. Prepare the planting hole as described earlier in the chapter and then place the tree in the centre of the hole with the stake positioned within 25–50mm (1–2in) of the tree trunk. Position the stake on the most convenient side of the tree. If near footpaths or roads, place the stake to protect the tree stem. In gardens, it is best to put the stake behind the stem as viewed

20 Driving in a stake before planting. A post-driver is very useful but steps and a sledge-hammer can be used

21 Placing the tree close to the stake and checking correct planting depth

22 Covering the roots with fine soil after spacing them out

23 Treading the soil firmly in all parts of the hole after covering the roots

24 One tree tie securely holding the tree to the top of the stake. A second tie may be required lower down

25 Covering the planting area with organic compost

from the house. Now set the tree aside and cover the roots with sacking while you drive the stake firmly into the ground. Ensure that the stake penetrates into undisturbed soil and is high enough to support the crown of the tree.

Return the tree to the hole and check the depth of the hole in relation to the correct planting depth. The union between root and stem should end up at the finished soil level. Too high and the roots will dry out, too deep and the moist soil could damage and rot the stem. If the hole is too shallow, excavate; if too deep, add soil. During this operation, the tree can be temporarily held to the stake with string or, better still, a second person can hold the stem of the tree.

Space out the roots carefully around the hole, ensuring that there are none twisting round the trunk. Then, with one person holding the tree, a second can commence back-filling with friable soil. Cover the lower fine roots first, ensuring that they are evenly covered by slightly lifting the tree up and down. Firm the soil gently with the sole of the foot. Continue back-filling and firming in this way until all the roots are covered. Ensure that the soil between the stake and the tree is firm, check that the tree is still at the correct depth, and then firm all round with the heel of the foot. Finally, fill and firm all parts of the hole with good soil to the surrounding soil level. Remove any excess soil and rake and tidy up the area.

It is important to plant the tree firmly. This ensures that all the roots are in contact with the soil and that there are no air pockets. On light, sandy soils you cannot over-firm with the feet, but on heavier clay soils be careful not to destroy the soil structure, particularly if the soil is wet.

The tree ties are now fixed in position. Place one tie within 25–50mm (1–2in) of the top of the stake and fix securely. Check that no part of the stem or branches is touching the stake. If the tree has a strong, straight stem one tie will be sufficient. If however, the stem is weak or bent, secure with a second tie approximately halfway down the stake or where the stem is touching or bowing.

Mulching materials can now be applied. If using the bulky organic materials, cover the entire tree-pit area 50–75mm (2–3in) thick. If using peat or other materials not containing plant foods, add two or three handfuls of slow-release compound granular fertiliser to the mulching material.

If using the 'Treespat', simply position it over the soil and around the stake and stem. Cover the edges of the spat with soil to prevent it blowing upwards or being caught by lawn-mower blades.

Guards, if required, can now be erected. The rabbit guards are simply placed around the stem

26 A 'Treespat' mulch fixed in position

27 Iron grille to allow access without soil compaction. This type must be removed early to allow for trunk expansion

28 This iron grille has a removable centre section to allow for trunk expansion

29 Concrete grille allowing water to penetrate but preventing compaction

30 Supporting a large tree with three stakes to avoid damaging the root ball

(see pls. 16 and 17). The 'Weldmesh' types are nailed or stapled to the stake leaving a gap at the base so that rubbish can be removed (see pl. 3). If larger cattle guards are needed, place these outside the tree pit, ensuring that the tree roots are not damaged (see pls. 18 and 19).

Grilles, if they are to be used, can be fitted at this stage, bearing in mind that they must be positioned so as not to damage the trunk.

Root-wrapped or container-grown trees

The planting of root-wrapped or container-grown trees follows the same sequence as for bare-root trees.

First remove the wrapping or container. Check and remove any small girdling roots. Keep the root ball intact and place the tree carefully in the planting hole. Again check the planting depth.

It is important not to damage the root ball by driving the stake through it. Therefore, it may be necessary to use two stakes driven in either side of the root ball with a crossbar nailed in position, or to drive the stake in at an angle to avoid the root ball. With larger root-balled trees three stakes may be required.

If there are small roots extending from the root ball these should be carefully spaced out and covered by the back-filling soil.

Larger root-balled trees

The critical points of planting advanced nursery stock and semi-mature sizes of trees are the same as for the smaller types, but it is first necessary to consider the more involved root-ball preparation, mechanical transportation and planting.

Root-ball preparation

Root-ball preparation is often necessary as the developing roots may otherwise extend too far from the trunk to be lifted.

If trees are purpose-grown from the nursery stock size in tree banks (see pl. 12) they should be regularly transplanted to encourage the growth of a mass of fibrous roots close to the trunk. This will not only provide sufficient young roots to continue to absorb water and nutrients but will also help keep the root ball firm when lifting and transporting. Some nurseries semi-containerise the roots by planting in polythene-lined wire cages. This allows some roots to pass through

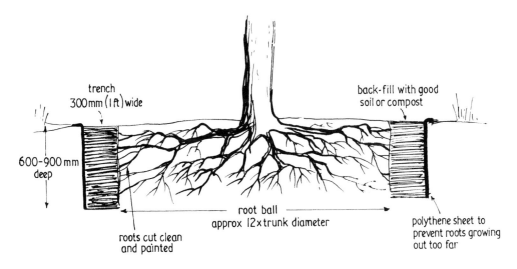

Fig. 11 Preparation of root ball by root pruning

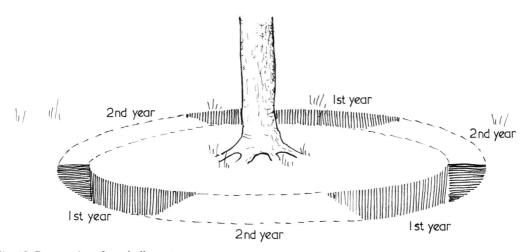

Fig. 12 Preparation of root ball over two seasons

into the surrounding soil, but the mass are kept within the container.

If the trees have not been regularly transplanted or grown in containers it will be necessary to induce fibrous-root growth within the root-ball area by root pruning a season or two before lifting.

First determine the size of root ball that can be safely lifted and that will support the tree. As a guide, the root ball should have a diameter twelve times greater than the trunk diameter, i.e. for every 25mm (1in) of trunk, allow 300mm (12in) of root ball. Mark this root-ball size around the soil and excavate a trench outside the line. The trench should be approximately 600–900mm (2–3ft) deep, depending on the size of the root ball, and 300mm (1ft) wide.

Any roots over 12mm ($\frac{1}{2}$in) in diameter should

be cleanly cut with a pair of secateurs or loppers and the cut ends sealed with a tree paint. To prevent the new roots growing outside the trench, a layer of polythene should be placed around the outer wall.

The soil is then returned to the trench and firmed. If the soil is poor it is better to replace it with good-quality loam or to improve it with organic materials such as peat or leaf-mould. Do not use strong manure.

This method of root-ball preparation is best carried out in the dormant period (October–March); the tree will then produce a mass of fibrous roots in the trench during the next growing season or two. During dry periods in the following summer it may be necessary to apply water to the trench area to encourage root development.

If the trees are very large it may be necessary to excavate the trench over two seasons. Divide the trench area into six segments and excavate alternate sections. Line the outer wall of each section and back-fill with good soil. The next season the remaining three sections can be dug out, lined, and filled as before. This more involved method has the advantage of not severing all the roots in one season, thus reducing the risk that the tree will suffer in dry periods; however, it requires careful marking because a year later it may be difficult to see where the first sections were excavated.

Once the root ball has been prepared and a mass of fibrous roots has developed in the trench area it is possible to lift and transplant the tree.

A second trench is excavated outside the original trench – the polythene lining will mark the area. The polythene can be removed and the loose soil carefully forked away to leave the mass of fibrous roots. These roots are vital for the tree's establishment, therefore they must be protected immediately by wrapping the entire root ball with hessian or canvas.

Lifting and transportation of large trees
Because of their size and weight, special lifting and transporting machinery will be required for large trees.

Advanced nursery stock trees up to 6m (20ft) high with a root ball up to 1m (3ft) in diameter can be lifted by an adapted fore-end loader mounted on a tractor. Larger semi-mature trees will require purpose-made machines. The Newman trailer works on a simple lever action with a lorry-mounted or Tirfor winch. More elaborate and expensive hydraulically-operated machines such as the American Michigan or the Vermeer Tree Space are also available in this country. Care must be taken to avoid damaging the root ball, and the branches should be tied in during transportation to prevent breakage.

Planting
Although mechanised, the planting must follow the same principles as for the smaller trees. Ensure correct planting depth, remove the hessian, space out the delicate fibrous roots carefully and back-fill and firm with good-quality soil.

Supporting
Because of their size and the necessity to prevent damage to the root ball, it is often necessary to use more elaborate supporting systems for large trees.

Staking
The advanced nursery stock trees may have been supported in the tree bank with a single stake. If this was the case it is possible to remove the stake stump and insert a larger stake in the original hole, taking care not to damage the branches when driving in the stake. Tie the tree to the stake as before with the larger-sized tree ties.

Alternatively, two or three stakes can be driven

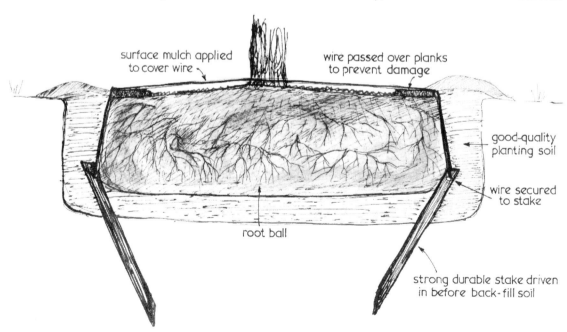

surface mulch applied
to cover wire

wire passed over planks
to prevent damage

good-quality
planting soil

wire secured
to stake

root ball

strong durable stake driven
in before back-fill soil

Fig. 13 Root-ball guying

31 Trees and shrubs planted in raised boxes. Very effective in soil-less sites, but trees require constant watering, as would a pot plant. Those shown here have a built-in irrigation system

into the soil outside the root-ball area and tied to the tree by means of a crossbar or with webbing or large tree ties (see pl. 30). If using the three-stake system, you will also be providing an effective cattle guard which can be made more effective by nailing wire netting or barbed wire around the stakes.

Guying

For the larger semi-mature trees, stakes may not be large or strong enough. Securing the crown of the tree with guy wires gives a very effective support system, but the wires may be a nuisance in lawns or pedestrian areas. They must not come into direct contact with the trunk, therefore some protection will be required. The wires can be passed through a short length of thick hosepipe, or slats of wood can be secured to the trunk first. The guy wires are secured by attaching them to wooden stakes or angle-irons driven into the ground.

Root-ball guying

Where overhead guys will create a nuisance, and where the root ball is solid, it is possible to anchor the tree by root-ball guying.

Before back-filling, stakes are driven into the

base of the planting pit and wires are secured to the stakes and passed over the root ball and down the stake the other side. To prevent the wire cutting through the roots, planks of wood are positioned on the top of the root ball.

This system can be very effective where you have a large solid root ball and a comparatively small crown. On very exposed sites and with tall trees, however, the unsupported crown could crack and break the root ball, and therefore overhead guying will be necessary.

Maintenance of Transplants

All transplants will require some after-care, but basically the smaller the tree the less the maintenance.

Irrigation
Owing to the fact that the roots must have been disturbed and damaged and that the planting site is often more exposed than the nursery, all trees will require a fair amount of soil moisture during the first season or two after planting. Average rainfall is often not sufficient and in dry periods irrigation will be essential. Watering the transplants with a watering can or hosepipe is easy enough in garden situations. Apply the water slowly and allow it to soak into the soil.

Where trees are planted in parks, on village greens or in the countryside, transporting water can be a problem. If large expensive trees have been planted in these situations a water tanker may have to be employed.

Trees planted in tubs or raised boxes are particularly vulnerable to drought and in certain cases it may be advisable to build an irrigation system into the planting area.

Checking supports and mulches
Regular checks should be made to ensure that the support system, guards, grilles, etc. are still effective and are not damaging the tree. This is normally done while irrigating and at the end of each growing season. Keep weeds clear of the tree-pit area. As the tree grows the ties will need adjusting to allow for trunk expansion. The mulching materials should be topped up at the end of each season.

Formative pruning
Any broken or damaged areas of the trunk or branches should be cleaned up or removed. All cut surfaces should be treated with a tree paint.

Consideration should be given to the shape of the crown of the tree. What are small branches now will be huge limbs in years to come. On the larger-growing trees retain one central leader and if there are two or three shoots competing for dominance remove the weaker ones. Keep the branch system well balanced and remove any crossing, weak or diseased branches. If access is required under the tree, remove the lower branches as the leading shoot develops.

Once the tree is established and growing (2–4 years) the stakes or supports may be removed. Ties and guys, if removed carefully, can be re-used. Stakes are best sawn off at ground level – to try to remove them could damage the roots.

6 Care of Existing Trees

There is no magical remedy or panacea to prevent or control all the troubles that can adversely affect trees, but basically we must all inspect our trees regularly and carry out any preventive or remedial treatments necessary.

In many cases we can just leave well alone. Trees growing in natural or semi-natural situations can often manage without the help of man. In urban road or park situations, however, we must be conscious of public safety, and tree inspections and maintenance work are a regular necessity.

Failure to recognise weaknesses in trees can result not only in the demise of the tree but also in the risk of prosecution if any part of the tree falls and damages property or injures people (see Chapter 11, Legal Rights and Responsibilities). Many tree owners will not have sufficient knowledge to recognise the various troubles or know how to correct them and may well need to seek professional guidance (see Appendix 1, Sources of Advice and Information).

When it has been decided that a tree requires attention it is then necessary to plan the execution of the task. Much of the work is potentially very dangerous for both the operator and surrounding features, and unless you are properly trained and equipped it is advisable to employ competent and fully insured contractors.

This and the following chapters give details of the various objectives and methods of tree inspections, pruning, remedial and preventative surgery and felling.

The Inspection

Every tree owner should regularly inspect his or her trees to see whether any repair work is required and also to check that the trees are not presenting a hazard to the public. Trees are best inspected twice a year, once when in leaf and again in the dormant season when the branch structure can be seen.

Before planning and deciding what can be done to protect our existing trees we must know where they are, their species, age, size and condition.

Position of trees
The situation of the tree and its surroundings will help us decide on any necessary action. If it is growing in woodland with no threat of disturbance we can normally leave well alone. Even if decayed and old, it is providing shelter and a habitat for wildlife. A similar tree standing by a road or building is a very different story (see pl. 56). If the tree or part of the tree fell the results could be disastrous. The owner could be liable for compensation to any damaged third party if the tree was showing obvious external symptoms of distress beforehand.

The planning department of the relevant local authority must be fully aware of the presence of good trees in its area. When there are plans for a change of land use or new developments they can consider the value of the existing trees and, where necessary, can legally protect them by Tree Preservation Orders.

Tree species
It is necessary to be aware of what types and forms of trees are growing, as some species will live longer and grow larger, some will be very prone to disease, others will tolerate root disturbance, pruning etc. Dense-foliage trees could create shade and leaf-litter problems; vigorous-rooting trees could undermine and damage buildings. Trees with poisonous leaves or fruit should not be retained in school grounds or near cattle.

The identification of trees and a knowledge of their form, qualities and disadvantages is a major study, but it can prove to be very interesting and rewarding.

Age of trees
The tree's age in relation to the normal lifespan of the species can be important when determining whether a particular tree is worth retaining. It is not always possible to be precise unless planting details are available but a rough method of calculation is to allow one year for every 25mm (1in) of trunk circumference. This simple rule is a fair guide to open-grown trees with a full crown. In woodlands, allow two years for every 25mm, and if in an avenue or small group or row allow one and a half years per inch. The circumference is measured at 1·5m (5ft) from ground level.

Knowledge of the tree's age, combined with observations on its present condition, will allow a judgement to be made as to its future life expectancy.

Size of trees

The existing dimensions of the tree will again indicate the age and life expectancy, depending on species. It will also clearly show whether the tree is going to create nuisance by giving too much shade or cause damage by its root spread.

Ideally any area or town should have a wide range of species, ages and sizes so that as the older trees have to be removed, there are others to replace them.

The height of a tree can be accurately measured with simple instruments or estimated by comparing with the height of a nearby feature, e.g. a double-decker bus, house etc.

Condition of trees

All parts of the tree are liable to damage and if damaged will show symptoms of distress. The destruction of the roots by excavation or disease will be indicated by the death of the leaves as the tree cannot absorb water. If the leaves are killed by fungus, insects or fire the tree will be weakened because it cannot manufacture its own food. Some symptoms are not so apparent; a tree could have an internal wood rot with no obvious external indications.

Thorough assessment of the condition of a tree can only be carried out by a fully trained arboriculturist who will know what is normally expected of a particular tree species and will recognise any abnormalities. However, every tree owner or person responsible for trees should check regularly for any obvious signs of trouble and call in experts where his own knowledge is limited, particularly when the trees are near to public areas. (See Chapter 12, Tree Disorders.)

Taking the various parts of the tree in turn, the main symptoms of trouble are as follows.

Leaves

The normal healthy leaf colour and size for the species should be known. If the leaves are discoloured, smaller than normal or dead it could indicate root problems or damage to the conductive tissues under the bark of the trunk or branches. There are a number of insect pests and diseases that eat or destroy the leaves, and the main types are described in Chapter 12. Healthy leaves do not, however, mean that the tree is sound. Internal wood rots that do not affect the living sapwood or the roots could render the tree very dangerous.

Twigs and shoots

Trees grow in height and spread by extending their leading shoots. General lack of shoot growth will indicate root or sap problems. A young vigorous tree will grow very quickly, but as the tree matures the growth will slow down. An abundance of dense shoot growth on the main trunk and branches could again mean root problems, though it could be the result of heavy lopping.

Branch system

The branch system gives the tree its overall shape and size. Some types are broad and spreading, others upright or fastigiate, while a few have branches hanging downwards to give a weeping habit.

The branch system should be evenly balanced and free from any dead areas of bark or rots and cavities. A very dense crown can be alleviated by careful pruning, but lopping off the ends of branches leaving stumps can result in vigorous re-growth and die-back. (See Chapter 7, Tree Pruning and Surgery.)

If branches are crossing and rubbing against one another, this can damage the protective bark and give rise to the entry of fungi and subsequent rots. Woodpecker holes are a clear indication of rots, as the bird is searching for insects which inhabit the decaying timber (see pls. 62 and 68). Old pruning scars are a common source of infection, particularly if the pruning was carried out by untrained staff and no tree paints were applied.

If any of the symptoms mentioned are observed it may require a climbing inspection to determine whether the branch is safe or could be repaired. This will normally mean employing a qualified tree inspector. If pruning is necessary, look out for any overhead power cables and telephone lines which may affect the work.

Binoculars are very useful for detailed inspection of the branches.

Trunk

The trunk of the tree acts as the main support for the branches, while the sapwood transmits food and water around the tree. The bark acts as a protective skin and prevents the entry of harmful organisms. If the bark is damaged it should be cleaned and repaired as soon as possible (see p. 69 and pls. 45 and 46).

The central part of the trunk is called the heartwood, and although it consists of dead tissue it still provides support. There are a number of fungus diseases that can enter and destroy this heartwood, thereby making the tree very unsafe. Sometimes these rots extend from open external cavities and can be seen quite clearly; others can develop and extend internally, the main sign of their presence being large fungal growths on the trunk or branches (see pl. 62). If these large fungal growths are seen, an advanced stage of internal decay is indicated, and again experts should be called in to determine the extent of the rot and to assess the tree's safety.

Internal examinations can be aided by the use of an auger or drilling device which, in experienced hands, can give a good idea of the tree's safety. An electrical meter is also being developed which will assist this examination process further.

Twin-forked or multi-stemmed trees can create problems. Tight upright forks do not have the strength of open rounded joints and often break off in gales. If the risk is recognised in time the tree surgeon can secure them by bracing (see Chapter 7).

Ivy on trunks does not do any real harm unless it becomes dominant in the crown, but climbing plants can hide cavities and rots and other dangerous symptoms, so they should be removed.

Root system

Although it is not possible to examine the roots, it is necessary to check the rooting area to see whether there are any indications of trouble. At the base of the trunk the main anchor roots will spread out. These can often be seen and checked for rots.

If the root area of the tree is open soil or supports other plants it will be possible to check for any signs of disease, toxic substances such as herbicides, road salt, or fire damage. Also check to see whether there has been any soil disturbance under the tree, for example trenches for services or alterations in soil levels or surfaces.

Recording information

The information gathered in the course of the inspection should always be recorded. If only a few trees are involved the recording can be done simply in a note and filed. Where large numbers of trees are involved a recording sheet can be used.

Many local authorities employ a system whereby the information is transferred to punched cards or even computerised for ease of retrieval and for work planning.

Where the inspector recognises that a tree is dangerous or that it requires further, more detailed examination, the necessary action should be taken without delay.

Chapter 11 covers the legal responsibilities for regular tree inspections and the role of the local authority concerning dangerous trees.

Example of Tree Inspection Recording Sheet

Site .... Date .... Inspected by ....

No	Species	Dimension		Age or Life Expectancy	Condition	Action
		Height	Spread			

7 Tree Pruning and Surgery

Skilful and judicious pruning and surgery not only make a tree safer but can also prolong its useful life. On the other hand, if carried out by unskilled or untrained staff they can very quickly spoil a tree's natural shape and be very dangerous for both operator and public.

Some of the operations mentioned here can be carried out by the properly equipped do-it-yourselfer, but for large trees, or where the tree is close to buildings, overhead cables or roads, only experienced, properly equipped staff or approved contractors should be used. (See Appendix 1, Sources of Advice and Information.)

Pruning

Pruning, or the removal of branches from a tree, is one of the most common and necessary operations. This is due mainly to the fact that in many towns and gardens we have inherited large-growing trees which are often too big for their situation, and pruning is one means of reducing

the problem without having to fell the tree. Since the procedure is irreversible and often expensive, always check that the work is necessary and justified. Most pruning operations can be carried out throughout the year, but avoid cutting birch, walnut and maple in the dormant season when they will bleed profusely and tree paints cannot be applied.

Reasons for and objectives of pruning
The problems which can be alleviated by pruning include large trees close to roads and buildings, trees containing dead or crossing branches, over-dense crowns, old pollarded trees and trees where the lower branches are blocking access ways.

British Standard 3998: 1966 defines the following pruning operations, together with the objectives.

1 Cleaning out
The removal of dead, dying or diseased wood and any other accumulated rubbish or debris from

32 Removing a large dead branch: a skilled and
    potentially dangerous job requiring properly
    trained and equipped professionals

33 Crude lopping spoiling the tree shape and resulting
    in vigorous re-growth and rots in the broken
    stumps

34 A vigorous willow creating problems because it is
     growing too close to a house

35 Careful removal of lower branches and reduction of
the density of the crown by thinning out weak and
crossing branches

the crown of the tree. Also includes the removal of unwanted climbing plants.

The objective of cleaning out or 'dead-wooding' is to remove dangerous dead or diseased wood so that it cannot fall to the ground and injure or damage people or property, and to help the tree by removing a source of likely infection.

2 Lifting of crown

The removal of the lower branches from the main trunk or branch system up to a specified height.

The obvious objective of crown lifting or 'raising the foliage' is to give greater access under or near to the tree. This is frequently necessary with street trees, and also where low branches are fouling footpaths or just blocking a view.

3 Crown thinning

The reduction of the density of the tree (not the overall dimensions) by removing weakly, thin and crossing branches and as many healthy branches as necessary to achieve the desired amount of thinning.

If carried out carefully by skilled staff this operation can diminish the very real problem created by large trees in small places, as it allows light and air into and through the crown. This reduces the weight of the crown, thus lessening wind resistance and making the tree safer.

Thinning is best carried out on the smaller end branches, not just by removing two or three large limbs from the central trunk (see pls. 34, 35).

4 Reducing and shaping

Reducing the height and/or spread of a tree by shortening the main branches to suitable points, leaving a shape as close as possible to the natural one. If 'crown reduction' is carried out carefully and all final cuts are back to growing shoots or other branches, a tree's dimensions can be reduced considerably without the kind of disfigurement which results from crude lopping or topping (see pl. 33).

The objectives are to reduce the height and/or spread where trees have outgrown their situation or where, because of rots or cavities in the branches or trunk, such reduction will make the tree safer. This work should only be carried out by experienced staff, and a ground man should guide the climber as to the best place to cut.

5 Crown renewal

Not a term used in British Standards, but a common operation where trees have previously been lopped or pollarded and the subsequent re-growth can now be thinned. This work can improve the appearance of a tree, but checks must always be made to ensure that the old lopping or pollard point is not decayed; it is only a short-term remedy, and regular checks and re-thinning will be required (see pl. 6).

Tools and equipment for tree pruning

For small tree work the following equipment will be required.

Hand saws with a fleam-tooth cross-cut tooth

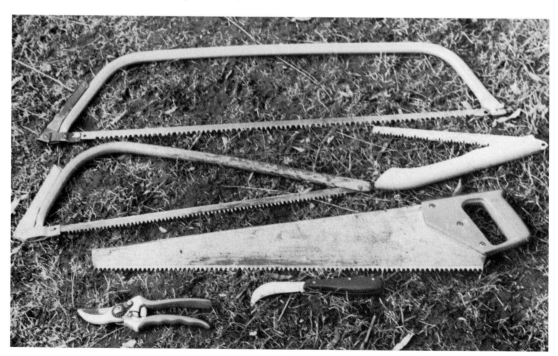

36 Hand pruning tools: bow saws, folding pruning
    saw, hand saw, secateurs and pruning knife

37 Medium and lightweight 2-stroke engine chain
    saws

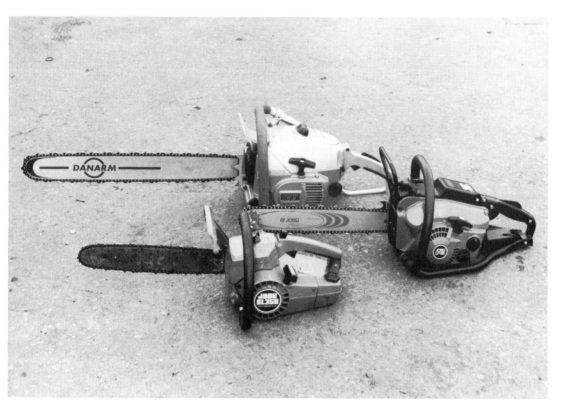

pattern can be purchased in the form of bow saws or conventional hand saws. Bow saws are cheaper and require no sharpening as the blades can be replaced. A 530mm (21in) bow is most suitable, but larger sizes are available.

Pole saws and extended loppers are very useful when only small branches – up to 37mm (1½in) diameter – need to be removed from ground level. When working with a metal pole saw, ensure that there are no overhead power cables in the vicinity.

Secateurs and hand loppers are useful for shrub and small tree pruning and can cut cleanly branches up to 12mm (½in) in diameter. A *pruning knife* will be useful for cleaning rough edges of cuts.

Tree paint will be required for sealing all cuts, particularly those over 25mm (1in) in diameter. A range of bitumastic types is available through garden centres, and one very useful and convenient method is the aerosol spray can: this is clean to use and there is little wastage. Tree paints act as a false bark to help prevent the entry of harmful organisms and stop the exposed tissue

drying out. However, they do not last for more than two to three years, and as large wounds will take many years to heal they should be re-painted regularly:

Working from *ladders* is potentially dangerous, and many accidents have been caused by using ladders in disrepair or failing to position and secure them correctly. Many people do not appreciate the size and weight of branches, or realise that if not cut correctly they can twist and fall on to the ladder. Use only stable ladders in good repair – there is a choice of metal, wooden and glass-fibre types available – and always have a second person with you to assist and to hold the ladder while you are ascending.

For small trees, step-ladders are useful, but ensure that the ground is firm or that the feet of the steps are resting on planks of wood.

For larger tree work the professional should use a *safety harness* and *nylon safety line*. This is a more involved system and should not be attempted by untrained staff (see pl. 32).

Chain saws are very efficient wood-cutting tools but in untrained hands are potentially lethal. A

range of sizes and types is available, from the very small electrically powered logging saw up to large direct-drive two-stroke engine saws for large tree felling. When selecting a saw, check that there is a good agent in the area for spares and servicing and read the instruction leaflet carefully. Never use a chain saw, particularly at height, without proper training.

There are a number of short training courses for staff involved in large tree work and chain-saw use: see Appendix 1, Sources of Advice and Information.

Small branch removal

All branches should be cut off carefully so as not unduly to damage the tree or important objects beneath. All final cuts should be into sound disease-free wood and made flush to the trunk or branch. To avoid tearing the bark under the branch, the branch should be removed by making three cuts.

The *first cut* is positioned approximately 300mm (1ft) out from the trunk and is made in the underside of the branch. Keep the saw horizontal and do not cut more than one-third of the way through the branch. If the cut extends further the branch could drop and jam the saw.

The *second cut* is made from above about 12–25mm ($\frac{1}{2}$–1in) further out along the branch. This cut should come down parallel to the first

38 Small electric chain saw, suitable for small cutting operations

39 Removing a small low branch with hand tools: first undercut to prevent branch tearing back. Position cut approx. 300mm (12in) from trunk. The ladder must be secured to the tree; and ensure that live power cables are at least 3m (10ft) clear of any part of the tree

40 The second (severing) cut is made from the top, 12–25mm ($\frac{1}{2}$–1in) further out along the branch. Ensure that the cuts are parallel to one another so that the branch will break off cleanly without twisting or tearing back towards the ladder

undercut, and when the two cuts are level the branch will break cleanly along the grain between them and fall to the ground without twisting or tearing. It is important to ensure that the cuts are parallel to each other.

The *third and final cut* is made flush to the trunk or branch to remove the small stump. If the stump is not long it can be cut off with one cut from top to bottom without tearing the bark. Although this final cut should be flush so as not to leave an ugly stump, it should not be made too flush on branches which swell out where they join the trunk. This over-flush cutting is more likely when chain saws are being used, and it results in a very large wound which will be more liable to invasion by wood-rotting fungi. All cuts over 25mm (1in) in diameter should be treated with a tree paint.

Small branches up to 75mm (3in) in diameter and no more than 4m (13ft) from ground level can be removed working from a ladder or steps and using hand pruning saws. Only use a ladder in good condition, and rest the top firmly against the trunk above the branch. If resting the ladder on a safe branch ensure that there are at least three rungs above the branch, for when the limb is severed and the weight lessened the remaining section of the branch will rise. The top of the

41 The third cut is made from the top and severs the stump flush back to the trunk. Do not leave stumps, but keep the wound as small as possible

42 Branches removed five years previously and cut flush enough not to look unsightly, with good healthy healing wood (callus) growing over the cut. The hatched line indicates the size of the cut if flushed off too close with a chain saw

43 Final cuts not flush enough, resulting in die-back, rots, and little or no callus formation

ladder should be secured to the trunk or branch with rope and the base footed by a second person or secured to a stake.

Larger branches will create many problems and dangers and should only be removed by professional staff using safety harness and a nylon safety rope and, where necessary, chain saws (see pl. 32).

Large branch removal
The pruning of large trees calls for a great deal of experience to ensure the safety of the operator, the public and any surrounding features.

Where branches can be severed and allowed to drop to the ground, the same three-cut method is used as for small branches. If there are other branches, features or fittings beneath the tree it will be necessary to take the branches off in smaller sections or by lowering them carefully with ropes. The climber will need to know the types of ropes and knots to use and must position the ropes over a higher strong fork and at the appropriate place on the branch so that the limb, once severed, can be held and lowered carefully by the ground man.

As with small branch removal, the final cut should be made flush with the trunk or branch and sealed with a tree paint.

Re-inspection of cut surfaces
Small wounds on vigorous trees will produce callus (healing wood) growth over the branch wound within a few years, with little chance of fungus organisms invading and causing rots. Larger wounds, however, will take many years to cover and some will never be completely sealed by the callus growth. The tree paints available at this time will give some protection for a few years, but large wounds should be re-painted every two or three years. If this is not done there is a very high risk of rotting.

Bark Wounds and Cavities

Many trees will develop rots and cavities in the roots, trunks or branches. The organisms that cause these rots often gain entry into the heartwood of the tree through damage to the protective bark. Unskilled tree pruning, animal or mechanical damage and storms are examples of injuries which, if left untreated, can extend into the heartwood of the tree and render it unsafe.

Once the rots have extended into the trunk or branch there is little that can be done to cure them. Therefore, it is necessary first to try and prevent damage; secondly, to clean and treat any

damaged area before rots develop; and thirdly, if
rots have developed, to determine their extent to
see whether the tree is unsafe or whether it can be
repaired.

Preventing damage

Prevention is always better and cheaper than
cure, particularly since, as already mentioned, it
is often not possible to eradicate all the rot.
Knowing the likely damaging agents, it is
possible to reduce the vulnerability of the tree by
the provision of effective protection.

Animals often remove and eat the bark,
particularly when bored or hungry. Stout fences
or guards will be required, particularly on
recently planted trees (see pls. 3, 16–19), if there
are cattle, horses, deer, sheep etc. in the area.
Smaller rabbit guards are also available, but only
select the stout tall types.

Grey squirrels can cause tremendous damage
to higher branches, particularly – but not
exclusively – on trees of the maple family. It is not
possible to fence them out, so if this pest is a
problem in your area it must be controlled (see p.
107 and Forestry Commission leaflet No 56, *Grey
Squirrel Control*).

Mechanical damage is very common, particularly
on roadside trees or in grass areas where the

44 Painting the cut with a tree paint to help prevent
rotting

45 Damaged area of trunk requiring treatment

46 Damaged area cleaned and shaped with a chisel
and given a liberal dressing of tree paint

careless lawn-mower operator will regularly knock into the trunk. Recently planted trees can be protected by guards or by keeping an area around the trunk clear of grass growth by mulching or the use of herbicides.

Do not use good trees for winch anchorage without providing adequate protection (see p. 79).

Storm damage cannot be prevented, but if limbs are broken off or the tree is struck by lightning it should be inspected and treated without delay.

Faulty workmanship – not cutting and sealing wounds properly – is a very common reason for the entry of wood-rotting organisms. The final cuts should be kept as small as possible and wounds must always be treated with a tree paint. Unfortunately, there is no tree paint available which will give lasting protection, and it will be necessary to re-paint large wounds every two or three years. If this is not done there is a very high risk of infection.

Treating freshly damaged areas
Where damage has occurred it is essential that the bark is cleaned back to sound, undamaged wood and the wound sealed.

A wooden or rubber mallet and an 18mm (1½in) carpenter's chisel are useful tools for cleaning and shaping bark wounds. Cut back to undamaged wood and keep the edges of the wound even to encourage callus growth. Where possible, shape the wound with the sap flow and slightly round off the top and bottom ends. Do not extend the wound any more than necessary and treat it with a heavy dressing of tree paint. Re-apply paint every two or three years until the wound has healed over.

Treating rots and cavities
Once a rot has extended deep into the trunk or branch there is little chance of cure. The fungus organisms which cause the rotting of the tissues will have extended much further than the obviously decayed area and complete removal of all the fungus will be impossible.

It is important to determine how far the rot has extended and for this reason it is often necessary to extend the access to the cavity. This can be done with a mallet and chisel, but a professional operator will use purpose-made tools – a chain saw or a powered rotary cavity-cleaning tool. Once greater access has been achieved, as much of the rotten wood as possible should be removed and burnt.

A fair degree of judgement and experience is required to determine whether or not the branch or trunk is still strong enough to be retained, but

if the rot extends for more than one-third of the diameter and the tree is in a public area it is best to remove the entire branch or fell the tree. If it is decided to retain the tree, the cavity should be treated with heavy dressings of tree paint to help prevent further infection. Remember, however, that the rots will continue to spread and further inspection and treatment will be required.

Until recently it was common practice to drill a 50mm (2in) diameter hole beneath deep cavities and to insert a drainage pipe. This allowed water to drain out and thus kept the area inside dry. However, research now suggests that this operation will extend the rot from the heartwood into the active sapwood; it should not therefore be practised.

Cavities should be left open to facilitate re-inspection and cleaning. The old practice of filling cavities with bricks or concrete did not support or help the tree, and the material was difficult to remove for re-inspection. Lightweight rigid foam fillers which are easily applied and removed are better, but they present a considerable health risk to the unprotected operator and are now rarely used.

If it is necessary to hide the hole, covering with fine wire mesh or hessian is much cheaper, and when painted the camouflage can hardly be seen.

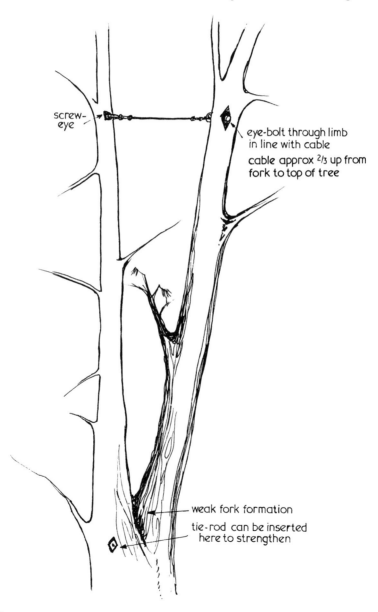

screw-eye

eye-bolt through limb in line with cable

cable approx 2/3 up from fork to top of tree

weak fork formation

tie-rod can be inserted here to strengthen

Fig. 14 Bracing twin-forked tree

Bracing and Propping

Where there are cavities in branches or weak-structured forks, or even if the whole tree is leaning, it is possible to prevent breakage or falling by supporting with cables or rod braces or by propping. It is first necessary, of course, to recognise the potential weakness.

Recognition of weaknesses

Some weaknesses are obvious and are comparatively easy to spot when inspecting trees; others may only be seen in a more detailed inspection or by the experienced tree surgeon. Obvious weaknesses that could be supported are:

1 Tight-forked or multi-stemmed trees
2 Heavy horizontal branches, especially spreading conifers, which will collect snow or catch wind
3 Branches weakened by cavities
4 Branches split or broken by storms
5 Leaning trees

Cable bracing

The weaknesses mentioned above have been recognised for many years, but the older methods of bracing relied on passing a metal collar around the trunk and attaching solid rods or chains. This evolved into the use of more efficient flexible cables, but these again were passed around the trunk and prevented from cutting into the bark by wooden slats. Neither of these now obsolete techniques allowed for trunk expansion, and the bracing materials would soon constrict and actually damage the trunk.

The modern method of bracing is to insert an eye-bolt or screw-eye through or into the trunk or branch and then attach the flexible cable. This system is comparatively simple, and it is useful for those responsible for trees to understand the principles, but the positioning of the bolts or screws and the cable tensioning is critical and should only be carried out by experienced staff.

Eye-bolts are inserted through the trunk or branch and a hole of the same diameter as the bolt is pre-drilled with a hand or power auger. A diamond-shaped washer is countersunk into the bark to prevent damage. Eye-bolts are more expensive than screw-eyes and take longer to install, but are required if the branch is weakened by rots or splits.

Screw-eyes are simply inserted into the branch. A hole of smaller diameter is pre-drilled and the screw-eye turned in. This is a cheaper method and is quite secure on sound limbs.

Galvanised round-strand cable, more commonly called multi-strand, is the best type of cable for bracing. It is flexible, strong and durable, and needs to be secured to the eye with bulldog grips.

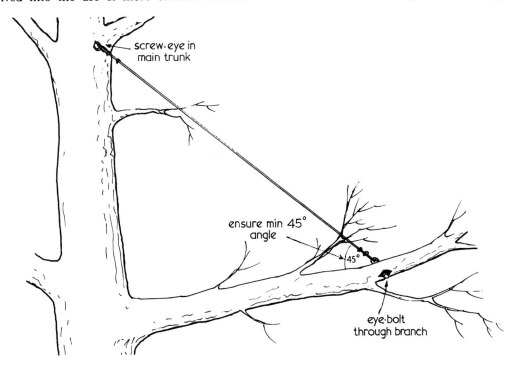

screw-eye in main trunk

ensure min 45° angle

45°

eye-bolt through branch

Fig. 15 Supporting heavy or weak branch by cable bracing

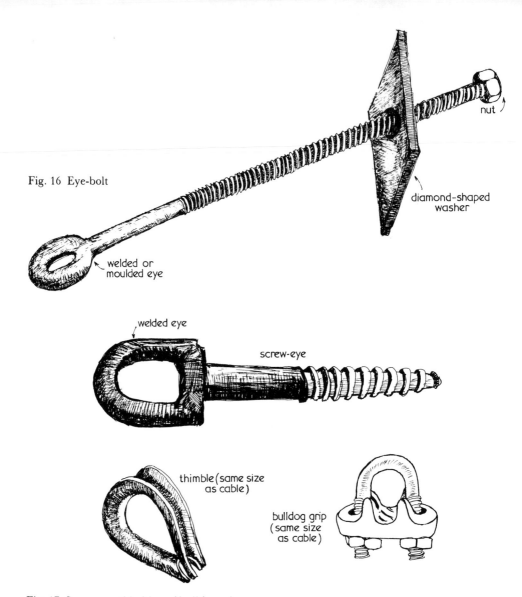

Fig. 16 Eye-bolt

nut

diamond-shaped
washer

welded or
moulded eye

welded eye

screw-eye

thimble (same size
as cable)

bulldog grip
(same size
as cable)

Fig. 17 Screw-eye, thimble and bulldog grip

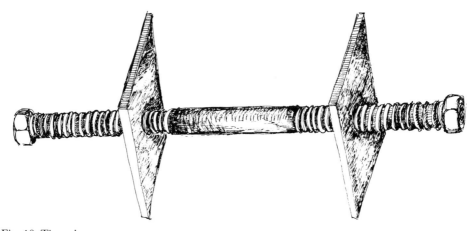

Fig. 18 Tie-rod

To prevent chafing, a metal thimble is inserted. Depending upon the size and weight of the branch being supported, a 5mm ($\frac{3}{16}$in), 6mm ($\frac{1}{4}$in) or 9mm ($\frac{3}{8}$in) diameter cable should be used.

Positioning of the cable to give maximum support is critical. This can only be judged by experienced staff, but as a rough guide, on twin-forked upright limbs position the cable approximately two-thirds of the way up from the fork to the top of the tree, and on horizontal limbs attach the cable as far out as possible in secure wood and ensure that the angle to the anchor point is at least 45°. If more than one cable is required they should be attached separately.

Tensioning of the cable is also vital. If at least one eye-bolt is used, the cable can be fixed hand-tight and then tensioned by tightening the nut against the washer. When using two screw-eyes, a small draw-vice tensioner is used. The cable should be tight enough to prevent any sag but not so tight as to distort the natural shape of the tree.

Rod bracing

Solid rod bracing should never be carried out high in the tree as it would create an inflexible situation and the whole tree could be weakened. However, where there are split branches, weak forks or cavities this method can be used to good effect to hold the damaged area together, thus preventing collapse.

Tie-rods constructed from 12mm ($\frac{1}{2}$in) diameter mild steel with a thread, washer and nut at each end are used. A hole of the same diameter as the rod is pre-drilled and the washer countersunk.

Position the rods to give maximum support; if this is done carefully they will not be seen, especially when the callus grows over the washer.

Propping

Propping branches, or in some cases entire trees, is only necessary when it is not possible to support by cables or rods.

Natural wooden props can be used, or alternatively they can be constructed from *timber* or *metal*. Make sure they are strong enough to give lasting support, but not so large as to create an ugly unnatural appearance. Some form of padding will be required between the prop and the live branch.

Position the prop to give maximum support; it must be rested on a strong base such as a concrete block or a paving slab.

Maintenance of the brace or prop is important. Although the actual supporting materials will last for many years without replacement, it is necessary to check regularly the original weakness, as this may have deteriorated so that the support is no longer effective.

Bracing and propping are very effective means of preventing damage, but must be carried out skilfully and do not give any guarantees. Therefore, if the tree is close to a busy public area, branch removal or felling should be considered to ensure public safety.

Tree Feeding

In natural woodlands trees obtain their nutrient requirements from the soil and there is a natural supply from the decomposing leaves. Where trees are growing in towns or in urban areas there is no natural return of nutrients as the leaves are either blown away or swept up. In such cases, and particularly on poor or compacted soils, the trees can suffer and may need help by application of manures or fertilisers or by breaking the compaction.

Recognition of deficiencies

Trees which are deprived of essential nutrients will show deficiency symptoms in the leaves. Leaves which are discoloured or smaller than normal or which show a general lack of vigour could indicate a shortage of available nutrients.

Positive nutrient tests can be carried out, and many garden centres and nurseries will stock simple soil-testing equipment. More detailed soil analysis can be carried out professionally and commercial enterprises can have their soil tested by the Agricultural Development and Advisory Service.

Feeding materials and their application

A range of materials can be used, but all should supply the nutrients slowly.

Bulky organic materials such as well-rotted manure, leaf-mould or garden compost are suitable. First break any compaction by light forking (be careful not to damage surface roots), and apply the material 75–100mm (3–4in) thick over the entire root area. If dry the soil should be thoroughly watered before applying the materials.

Concentrate fertilisers have the advantage of less bulk and mess but if applied only to the top of the soil could be used up by surface-rooting plants or lost by water run-off. It is, therefore, necessary to insert the fertiliser into pre-drilled holes: 50mm (2in) diameter holes are drilled 600mm (2ft) apart and 300mm (1ft) deep over a band extending 1·5m (5ft) to either side of the outer limit of the branch spread.

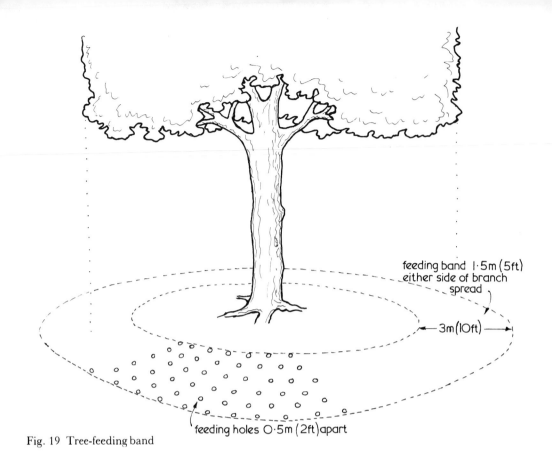

feeding band 1·5m (5ft) either side of branch spread

3m (10ft)

feeding holes 0·5m (2ft) apart

Fig. 19 Tree-feeding band

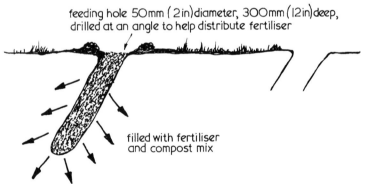

feeding hole 50mm (2in) diameter, 300mm (12in) deep, drilled at an angle to help distribute fertiliser

filled with fertiliser and compost mix

Fig. 20 Detail of tree-feeding hole

The amount of fertiliser per hole will vary according to soil type and the size, health and vigour of the tree but, on average, allow 100–150g (3½–5oz) per hole. It is preferable to bulk up the fertiliser with sand or fine compost. Compound granular slow-release fertilisers are best and are available from garden centres and nurseries.

Seasons for application
The bulky materials can be applied at any time of the year, but ensure that the soil is in a moist condition.

Compound fertilisers are best applied from spring to early summer. At this period the tree will be able to make use of nutrients. If applied later in the summer, they may produce lush growth which could be damaged by autumn weather; if applied in winter, much will be lost by drainage before the tree can utilise the nutrients.

Further and more detailed information on tree pruning, surgery and felling is available in a companion book, *Tree Surgery: A Complete Guide*, published by David & Charles in 1976.

8 Tree Felling

Trees, like all other life forms, have a natural safe life cycle. They grow, mature, decline and eventually die. At any point in this cycle they could become dangerous, be in the way of developments or be felled for their timber values.

Tree felling, then, is part of the cycle or management plan. We simply remove the trees before they fall and cause damage or in order to utilise the valuable timber. Any properly managed maintenance programme should include felling, and the trees will not be unduly missed if there are others growing nearby.

Not all tree felling, however, is justified. We see far too many trees removed unnecessarily. Chapter 11 deals with the legal constraints on felling, but in addition it is necessary to justify the expense of felling and the loss of amenity.

Reasons for Felling

In urban areas and where trees are close to roads, buildings or public rights of way the owner has an obligation to ensure public safety. If any weaknesses are recognised early, they can be corrected by pruning or surgery, but sometimes the only safe course of action is to fell. Dutch elm disease is one example of a disease that will very quickly kill even large trees, and there are many other similar troubles which mean that trees must be felled for safety reasons or in order to prevent the disease spreading to other trees (see Chapter 12, Tree Disorders).

We need more land for roads and buildings. In some cases trees can be successfully retained (see Chapter 9, Care of Trees on Development Sites), but inevitably others will have to go and new ones should be planted in more appropriate places. With land prices escalating, more homes are built per acre, therefore fewer trees can be retained.

Trees also provide a vital material – timber. It is not the intention of this book to discuss commercial forestry, but where landowners have a management plan for their estate, tree felling for timber can be justified. If trees are left long past maturity their timber value may well be lost.

Farmers are the main custodians of our countryside, and it is thanks to them that we have inherited such a beautiful and varied landscape. However, in many areas tree and hedgerow clearance has been overdone, resulting in loss of amenity and shelter and the creation of dust-bowls.

Tree felling, then, must be justified. It is not acceptable to fell simply because of leaf nuisance, too much shade on the vegetable patch or because a developer can build just one more house. The existing legislation is not watertight, and we need even greater public awareness and consideration for others if we are to prevent unnecessary tree removal.

Methods of Felling

Once felling has been agreed upon it is necessary to consider how it should be carried out. Felling even small trees is fraught with danger and professional expertise will normally be required. Thought must be given to the direction of fall, whether or not the stump is to be removed, disposal of branches and timber, and tool and equipment requirements.

Small tree felling

Trees up to 300mm (1ft) in trunk diameter and 10m (33ft) in height can be felled with basic hand tools – small chain saws and/or portable hand winches. If the tree can be felled to ground level and the stump left, the method is as follows. First determine the direction of fall; this should be with the natural weight or lean of the tree. If the tree is evenly balanced and there are no surrounding features, fell in the direction most convenient for clearance. When the tree is leaning in the wrong direction it will be necessary to reduce the weight on the heavy side (see Branch Removal in Chapter 7).

Once the direction of fall has been determined, it is advisable to attach a pulling rope as high as possible in the crown of the tree. This is required to give the tree its initial momentum in line with the intended direction of fall. Clear all branches and debris at the base of the tree to avoid tripping and decide on an escape route in case of emergencies.

The first cutting operation is to remove a wedge or 'sink' of wood from the base of the tree. This sink should be positioned as low as possible and at right-angles to the direction of fall. The removal of the sink requires two cuts. The first

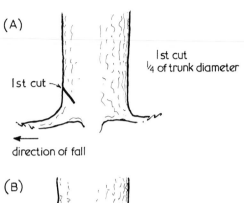

(A)

1st cut →

1st cut
¼ of trunk diameter

direction of fall

(B)

2nd cut →

45°
angle

2nd cut meets up with
base of 1st cut.
Section of wood ('sink')
removed

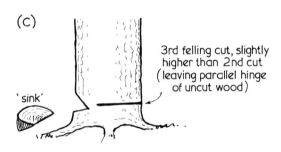

(C)

'sink'

3rd felling cut, slightly
higher than 2nd cut
(leaving parallel hinge
of uncut wood)

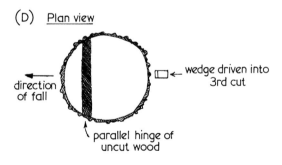

(D)   Plan view

direction
of fall

wedge driven into
3rd cut

parallel hinge of
uncut wood

Fig. 21 Tree-felling cuts

cut should be made downwards at an angle of 45°
and should penetrate to approximately one-
quarter of the trunk diameter. The second cut is
made horizontally to meet up exactly with the
base of the first cut (see pl. 47). It is important to
ensure that the two cuts meet up exactly so the
wedge of wood can be removed and a straight line
maintained to give a clean fall. A third, severing
cut is then made from the back of the tree. This
cut must be made at the same height as or slightly
higher than the sink cut, ensuring that it is
parallel to the sink. Do not cut right through; the
object is to leave a parallel strip of uncut wood
between the back of the sink and the severing cut.
This uncut strip will act as the hinge to give a
clean straight fall. The thickness of the hinge will
vary according to the type of tree and the crown
weight, but leave approximately 35–50mm
(1½–2in) of uncut wood. If the tree starts to crack
or move while you are making the cut, remove the
saw and retreat.

A steady pull on the rope will now give the tree
its initial movement. When pulling, ensure that
you are farther back than the height of the tree,
and do not allow the tree to rock back on the
hinge, or it could fall in the wrong direction. If the
hinge does not break on the first pull, release the
rope and cut slightly more. A felling wedge can be
driven into the back of the severing cut to aid the
initial movement.

When felling, always check that there are no
children, pets or helpers in the vicinity of the fall.
Also watch out for dead or broken branches in
the tree which could fall straight down.

Once the tree is down it can be cut up into
convenient lengths for disposal. Remove the
pulling rope and first cut off all clear branches.
Do not attempt to cut branches under tension as
these could spring up or jam the saw. Once all the
free branches are cleared, roll the trunk over and
remove the remaining limbs. If on sloping land,
always try to work on the uphill side of the trunk,
as it could roll when the branches are removed.

Felling large or difficult trees
The felling of large trees and trees standing close
to roads, buildings etc. should only be attempted
by experienced staff or fully insured contractors.
The same basic methods are used, but because of
the size of the trunk and the weight of the tree,
chain saws and power or hand winches will be
required.

Professional operators will check all
surrounding features and hazards and again
determine the direction of fall. Cutting with
chain saws is very quick and efficient but there is
little room for error. It is quite common to find

47 A properly protected professional operator felling a large tree with a chain saw. He is removing the 'sink' slightly higher than normal because of internal basal rot

old fence wire or nails in the trunk, and if, when cutting the sink, it is found that the base of the tree is hollow or rotten, other methods of felling may have to be adopted.

Leaning trees also present problems. Even if the tree can be felled with the lean the trunk could split as the back severing cut is made. If it is essential to fell a leaning tree in the other direction it will be necessary to employ large tractor- or lorry-mounted winches or occasionally to fell the tree in sections. Dismantling the tree in sections requires a great deal of experience. It means cutting and lowering branches and sections of trunk with ropes. With large trees professional operators will use chain saws at height in conjunction with safety harnesses.

Trees half-fallen and suspended in other trees or over buildings again present many problems and dangers. The trunk will be under tension and could snap or roll when cutting commences. For very large trees it may be necessary to hire cranes to lift and pull the tree clear.

Such work should never be undertaken by untrained personnel.

Timber Removal

Few people realise the volume and weight of trees until they are on the ground, and branch and trunk removal or disposal can create difficulties.

Burning on site is a very efficient means of disposing of branches and small trunks and stumps but in certain areas the clean air regulations will prohibit this. If burning is permitted the fire should be carefully controlled and, in public areas, extinguished before you leave the site. Never light fires when the surrounding vegetation is dry, or on peaty soils.

Where fires are prohibited alternative means of disposal must be found. Carting away and tipping is possible but some refuse tips will not permit loose brushwood tipping. Brushwood chipping machines are available and many large local authorities and firms use these. They reduce the volume of loose branches to one-fifteenth of their original bulk and the chippings, if disease-free, can be decomposed and used as compost or mulch. If the stump or roots are diseased or obviously rotten the chips should be burned or disposed of well clear of existing trees.

Where several trees are being felled it may be worth investigating the possibility of selling the timber, even if just for firewood. Large sound trunks could be worth a considerable amount of money, and if there is access for a lorry, timber merchants will come and pick up and pay for the timber. The price paid will vary according to the type of tree and the volume of the timber.

48 Range of Tirfor winches and ancillary equipment

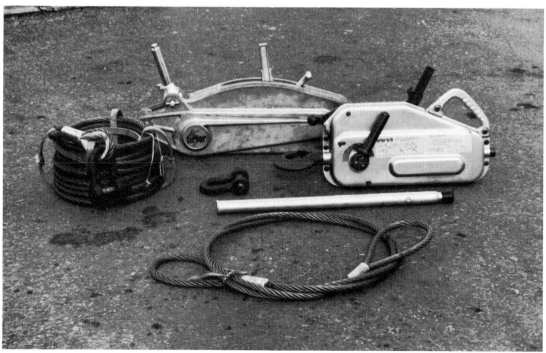

Stump Removal

Where trees are felled to ground level there is still the problem of removing the stump and the main roots. It is possible to pull the whole tree over together with the stump, but this will require the use of hand or power winches.

Small trees can be pulled over with a comparatively small portable hand winch. The Tirfor range of winches is very suitable for this. The Tirfor TU16 will safely pull 1½ tonnes (tons) and the larger model, T35, will pull 5 tonnes (tons). These winches can be purchased or hired but, although they are basically simple to operate, training is required to set up the pulling system.

A strong anchor is needed to secure the winch, and this must be positioned at a distance from the tree which is greater than the tree's height. Nearby trees can be used, but check that the anchor tree is strong enough and, if that particular tree is to be retained, protect the trunk from cable damage. On rough-barked trees lengths of solid branch can be inserted between the anchor cable and the tree, but if only smooth, easily damaged trees are available, give additional protection such as sacks packed with twigs or straw. Purpose-made ground anchors are also available.

The pulling cable is attached to the trunk of the tree which is to be pulled over. It should be attached as high as possible, but on wood which is strong enough to take the strain of the pull without breaking. Before pulling, excavate a trench around the trunk and sever any large roots.

Large trees will require heavier, more dangerous equipment, and this is another operation which should only be attempted by experienced staff. Tractor- or lorry-mounted winches are used or, on open sites, a bulldozer can first cut off the main roots and then push over the tree.

Where trees are cut off at ground level there are alternative ways of removing the stump.

Winches – either the small hand winch for small trees, or a tractor-mounted winch for large stumps – can be used. As there is no trunk to which the pulling cable can be attached, there is not so much leverage, and more root cutting will be required. But the stump still remains to be disposed of, and this can be difficult. Burning is slow and removal by lorry is expensive. Therefore the other methods of stump removal should be considered.

Blasting can be a very efficient method so long as experienced contractors are employed. If the charges are positioned correctly the blast will not only lift the stump out of the ground but break it into smaller pieces for easier disposal. This operation can only be carried out on large open sites.

Burning the stump *in situ* is a very slow and smelly method. Saltpetre and paraffin can be poured into slits or holes in the stump surface and ignited once they have soaked in. Do not use this method on peaty soils, as in dry conditions the peat will burn and smouldering will slowly spread underground.

Chemicals can be used to kill the stump; this will prevent sucker growth but, contrary to some claims, it will not remove the stump. Total persistent weedkillers such as sodium chlorate or ammonium sulphamate are used. To prevent spillage into surrounding soil the chemical crystals are inserted into pre-drilled holes or slits in the sapwood of the stump.

Stump-cutting machines are probably the most efficient means of stump disposal, provided there is suitable access (1·3m (4ft) for the smallest machine). The cutter reduces the stump to small chips which can easily be disposed of or spread on site. These machines are available for hire, with operator, in many parts of the country. The hire charge will depend on the number of stumps to be removed and the distance of the site from the hire company's depot.

9 Care of Trees on Development Sites

Trees are often felled to make way for new buildings, roads etc, or otherwise adversely affected by construction work. In some cases, felling is necessary where new developments are required, but all too often trees are removed without good reason or insufficient thought is given to the effect of the building works on the trees. The subsequent removal of the dead trees after development may be much more expensive than clear felling in the first place.

It is also important to appreciate that trees can, in some circumstances, adversely affect buildings.

Effects of Developments on Trees

Many developers either forget that trees are living plants and have roots, or knowingly destroy the trees to make way for further buildings. All new development requires planning permission, and it is at the outline planning application stage that the local planning authority should investigate the existence of trees and, where necessary, protect them by planning constraints or by Tree Preservation Orders (see Chapter 11, Legal Rights and Responsibilities).

The effect of the building on existing trees will depend greatly on the species, age and health of each tree and the proximity of the site works. In principle, the younger and more healthy and vigorous the tree the better it will be able to withstand disturbance, particularly to its root system. Mature trees, especially oak, beech and many conifers, are very vulnerable and they will die or become dangerous if the root systems are unduly disturbed.

Alterations to site soil levels and surfaces are the most common cause of suffering in trees. Most of a tree's roots are located within the top 1m (3ft) of soil, and the delicate fibrous roots are mainly within 300mm (1ft) of the surface. Therefore, any lowering or raising of soil levels can seriously affect the tree's stability and its ability to absorb water.

Ideally, no changes of soil levels or surfaces should be carried out within the crown spread of the tree. If it is necessary to lower levels close to the trunk, this should be done with care and a retaining wall should be erected to protect the remainder of the roots. Where it is necessary to raise levels, only good-quality porous soil should be used. If a hard surface is required under part of the tree, use porous non-toxic materials.

The rainwater catchment area of the tree can be dramatically reduced by lowering soil levels even some distance from the tree, and in dense housing areas much of the rainwater is diverted into storm drains and lost to the soil. In such cases even large trees may require irrigation in dry periods.

Site works can also have detrimental effects on trees. All building materials should be stored away from the trees, particularly subsoil, fuel and chemicals. No fires should be allowed anywhere near the trees, and all parking sites and access routes should be kept well clear of the roots.

Effects of Trees on Buildings

Despite all the attractions of trees and their value among buildings, it is important to consider their possible detrimental effects. The two main areas of concern are the nuisance of trees too close to houses and the actual risk of structural damage.

Nuisance can be used as an excuse for unnecessary felling, but large trees in small gardens do cause problems, with too much shade to the house or garden, leaf litter blocking gutters and drains, and the risk of the tree falling or branches breaking off in gales. Trees can also create problems with neighbours and can lead to common law disputes (see Chapter 11).

Structural damage is a far more serious threat, but is only a real problem where large vigorous trees are retained close to buildings on shrinkable clay soils (see pp. 29–30, 93–4).

49 Trees marked for retention but inadequately protected, resulting in severe root damage and likely death of the trees

50 Vehicular access and storage of materials under retained trees resulting in soil compaction and root damage

Tree Surveys

To avoid the risk of damaging trees or of trees creating problems, it is necessary to site new developments, as far as possible, clear of the existing trees. When any development is planned, therefore, it is important to be fully aware of the presence, size, species and condition of any trees on site. For small home extensions this can be done quite simply, but if the intention is to build a number of houses or to construct a new road where there are existing trees, it will be necessary to carry out a detailed tree survey.

Ideally the survey should be made before any building location plans are decided, then the houses, roads etc. can be so sited as to avoid the good trees. All the existing trees should be plotted on a scale drawing (1:500 or 1:1250); it is important to ensure that the actual positions of the trunks are accurately recorded. The trees can then be numbered on the plan, and, if necessary, corresponding metal tag numbers can be attached to the trees themselves. At this stage a schedule can be drawn up and the details of each tree recorded.

Example of Tree Survey Schedule

Site .... Date .... Surveyor ....

| Tree No | Species | Dimensions | | Age | Condition | Surrounding features | Category |
		Height	Spread				
1	Oak	20m	18m	100 yrs	Healthy Minor dead wood	Open ground	A
2	Beech	22m	19m	100 yrs	Dead wood in upper crown. Some small decay in trunk	10m from existing road and ditch	C
3	Horse Chestnut	15m	10m	70 yrs	Healthy. Pollarded at 5m 20 years ago	Open ground to west, road 6m to east	B
4	Ash	17m	8m	70 yrs	Major rots in base of trunk		D

Tree species can often be recorded by the common or English name, but where a number of species of the same genus are present it may be necessary to use the botanical name (see Chapter 2).

Tree dimensions are important to relate to the proximity of any proposed buildings, and they should be accurately measured. Simple instruments are available for this. More detailed surveys may require trunk diameter, the spread of the branches as a radius from the trunk and the amount of clear stem or branch clearance from ground level.

Age is not always easy to determine without experience, but as a rough guide an open-crown tree will have 25mm (1in) of trunk circumference (measured at 1·5m (5ft) from ground level) for every year of its life. Therefore a tree 2m (6ft, or 72in) in circumference will be about seventy years old. If trees are growing close together, say in woodland, allow two years for every 25mm (1in); allow for variations too where trees are growing in avenues or in small well-spaced groups.

The condition of the tree is very important, as this will be directly related to its tolerance of disturbance and the dangers that might result if houses are built close to it. The obvious signs of danger and the necessity for tree inspections are covered in Chapter 6.

Surrounding features are worth noting, as again they will guide in the plotting of buildings and necessary site works. Note a tree's proximity to existing roads, buildings, ditches, power cables etc.

The *tree category* is a useful final judgement on each tree. Trees can be grouped into three, four or five categories, as follows:

Category A: Important trees in good condition

Category B: Less important visually, but otherwise sound

Category C: Suspect trees with major dead wood or rots in trunk or branches (may require more detailed inspection)

Category D: Dead, dying or obviously dangerous trees

Category E: Transplantable trees

On large-scale sites, with many trees, it is often an advantage to link the categories to a colour code and, say, colour the 'A' trees green, 'B' yellow, 'C' blue, 'D' red and 'E' brown. By colouring the trees on the plan you obtain an immediate visual impression of the overall site. Areas with many 'A' or 'B' trees can be kept clear of developments, while buildings, roads etc. can be sited in 'C', 'D' and 'E' areas.

Site Planning

Once armed with the detailed tree survey the architect, developer, planner etc., in conjunction with an arboriculturist, can finalise the site layout and decide which trees can safely be retained and which are to be removed.

All the details of the buildings should be considered, including houses, garages, hard-

51 A fence erected before site works commenced giving effective protection to tree and roots

surface areas such as paths and roads, sewerage and drains, services and so on. Space should be agreed for site huts, storage areas, parking and temporary access routes. If demolition is necessary, fire sites and disposal areas should be clear of the retained trees. On sites with limited space the storage of some materials may be permitted under or near to the trees, but only in the case of non-damaging items such as timber, window frames and small fittings.

Tree protection

Before any site works commence it will be necessary to protect the retained trees. This should be carried out physically, by the provision of strong barrier fences, and, if necessary, legally, by Tree Preservation Orders (see Chapter 11). The barrier fences should be constructed of strong durable materials which will not easily be broken, and should be erected as far out from the trunk as possible. Ideally the barrier should be placed as far out as the branch spread on broad-crown trees or the equivalent distance on upright trees. Where trees are growing in groups or rows, it is better to enclose them all within a single barrier.

Tree clearance

Once the retained trees have been protected, the unwanted trees can be removed. Care should be taken to avoid damage to the existing trees, and fire sites particularly should only be permitted at a safe distance.

Site Supervision

Despite the good intentions of the planners it is still the digger operator who will be on site and perhaps causing damage. The clerk of works or site foreman should know about the retained trees, and regular site visits by qualified arboricultural staff will also be necessary. The retained trees and their protective barrier fences should be checked periodically, particularly if there is an extended building programme.

On completion of the main building programme there will be the final landscape treatments. Many landscape contractors will be fully aware of the need to protect and retain trees, but others may still cause damage when the barrier fences are removed for ground contouring, grassing and planting.

The retained trees should be checked for any signs of damage and remedial surgery carried out where necessary.

Planting

To give continuity to the treescape, consideration should be given to planting trees. Selection and siting will be important, and money should be allowed for maintenance (see Chapter 5).

10 Woodlands, Hedgerows and Shelter Belts

Woodlands once covered most of the United Kingdom. Very few, if any, of these natural ecosystems survive today. What woodlands there are fall into two main categories:

1. Managed woodlands where the primary objectives are timber and/or amenity
2. Derelict or, neglected woodlands often with high amenity and wildlife value, but little timber use

Most of our field hedgerows were created as a result of the Enclosure Acts of the last three centuries. Many thousands of miles of hedgerows have now been removed to make larger and more efficient field sizes, while those that are left are often cut by mechanical tractor-mounted machinery, which means that few, if any, tree seedlings can survive. Garden hedges fulfil many useful and decorative functions but require regular maintenance.

Shelter belts have been introduced in comparatively recent times because of the loss of protection through the removal of woods and hedgerows. Their functions, size and composition are variable, but they can provide not only shelter but amenity and variety in the landscape.

Woodlands

Although woodlands now cover only a fraction of the total land area, they are still important landscape features, providing shelter for farm crops and animals and, depending on the trees present, affording protection and habitat for a variety of wildlife. They can also provide a very pleasant environment for active and passive recreational pursuits, and, most important, the trees can supply a vital renewable raw material – timber. This book is not concerned with commercial forestry purely for the production of timber, but as the forestry areas are there for many decades they can also fulfil amenity functions, while even small, so-called amenity woodlands can produce a sustained supply of timber if properly managed.

Commercial woodlands

Most woodlands can produce usable timber and, therefore, can often attract grant aid. Any woodland owner should at the outset contact the Forestry Commission's Conservator of Forest for his area. Forestry Commission staff will advise on the suitability of any scheme and will also suggest the most appropriate form of grant aid.

The preparation of a plan of operations, the actual planting, fencing, drainage etc. and the sale or utilisation of timber may be beyond the scope of the owner. However, there are a number of consultants and contractors who specialise in this type of work and can advise not only on timber production but also on other woodland uses such as game, wildlife and recreation.

There are also two woodland owners' associations: the Timber Growers' Organisation, covering England and Wales, and the Scottish Woodland Owners' Association in Scotland.

For addresses of the Forestry Commission, consultants and contractors and woodland owner associations, see Appendix 1, Sources of Advice and Information.

Amenity woodlands

To class a woodland purely as an amenity is incorrect. In fact some of the best amenity woodlands are those where there is a sound timber-production policy. However, if woodlands, particularly those owned by local authorities, are to be opened to the public, this use can conflict with forestry policy and create dangerous situations.

In large woodlands it is often possible to segregate the public from the sensitive forestry areas by inviting people into certain areas. It is better to welcome the walkers, horse-riders, campers etc. into clearly defined areas than to say 'Keep Out!' Where they are made welcome and provided with parking and other facilities they will use them and should not stray into the areas where planting or timber extraction is being carried out.

Many private woodlands do provide such facilities, which can provide much-needed income between planting and harvesting. Forest guides, nature trails and such activities as orienteering can be organised, thus helping to meet the educational and sporting needs of the area.

Shooting and fishing are also very popular sports which can often be accommodated within

the forest area, but care must be taken to ensure that such activities do not conflict with its use by the general public.

Derelict or neglected woodlands

There are still many large and small areas of old neglected woodland, many of which are in private ownership. Such woods with their decaying and fallen trees can provide habitats for a variety of wildlife, and some ought to be left well alone as a refuge. However, depending on the soil type and the condition of the trees present, some will, if not managed properly, fall into complete dereliction and demise. Others could be slightly improved by cleaning drainage ditches and clearing rides for access without spoiling the wildlife habitat unduly. Such areas can provide ideal projects for local groups or schools, either as clearing and tidying operations or for natural history studies.

Fire protection

One of the most serious threats to woodlands, particularly young plantations, is fire. The chief officers or firemasters of local fire brigades provide a free advisory service with regard to fire prevention and control (see Appendix 1).

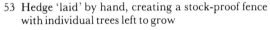

53 Hedge 'laid' by hand, creating a stock-proof fence with individual trees left to grow

Hedgerows

Trees and shrubs on field boundaries and roadsides and in gardens fulfil a variety of functions and provide many attractions. They frame the patchwork pattern of our typical landscape, provide shelter for farm crops and stock, and form the habitat for all manner of wild fauna and flora.

The sprawling unkempt hedge propably provides the best attractions and habitats, but it can take up a disproportionate amount of valuable farmland. Careful cutting with hand tools, leaving the strong growing seedling trees, created our pattern of hedge-with-trees. Skilful hedge laying to create strong stock-proof fences is unfortunately practised now in only a few areas.

The mechanical tractor-mounted cutting machines are crude and cannot discriminate between hedge plant and young tree. Owing to economics, this method of controlling the spread and height of hedges is now the most common, and is perhaps better than no hedge at all. With a little more care, though, good young trees could be retained, for instance, by marking them so that the tractor driver can lift his machine around them.

Over the past years many thousands of miles of hedgerows have been removed to create larger, more economic field sizes. Government grant aid was available for this operation, and in places it was drastically overdone, spoiling the landscape and creating dust-bowls, particularly on light soils, and allowing deep snowdrifts to form on the roads in winter. In some areas farmers are now having to re-plant.

The burning of straw and stubble is commonly practised, and if not carried out with care this can easily destroy hedgerows. The National Farmers' Union issues a *Straw and Stubble Burning Code* (see Appendix 1) which, if followed, should reduce the hazard.

Garden hedges are of tremendous value in towns. They can provide a variety of attractive features depending on the species selected, form effective barrier screens between properties for privacy and shelter, and are probably the most important source of food and nesting sites for birds.

There is a vast range of trees and shrubs that can be planted to form hedges in both town and country. In rural areas preference should be given to locally growing species such as hawthorn, blackthorn, spindles, Viburnums, field maple, bramble etc. These can be clipped to control their height and spread or left wild to form hedges of natural-looking appearance.

54 Mechanical tractor-mounted hedge-cutting operation – efficient, but it allows no young seedlings to develop into hedgerow trees

55 Formal clipped beech hedge providing shelter, screening and all-the-year-round amenity

Good-quality, feathered trees and shrubs should be planted in single rows with 600mm (2ft) between plants, or in double rows with 900mm (3ft) between plants and the rows 600mm (2ft) apart, the second row staggered with the first.

On exposed sites only small sturdy stock should be used and some form of permeable fence may be required until the plants are established. In extreme conditions, such as those found on the coast, the range of plants that will establish is more limited. On the north coast of Cornwall, for example, only shrubs like Escallonia, Elaeagnus, Oleria, Hippophae and Senecio will tolerate the salt-laden gales.

In gardens a great variety of trees and shrubs can form formal clipped hedges or loose spreading flowering screens. Evergreen or deciduous types can be used and, if properly maintained, particularly in the early formative years, can provide all the qualities of a living wall. Hedges in fact form much better windbreaks than, say, brick walls or solid fencing, as the wind is filtered through the barrier rather than diverted over or round it (see fig 22). (Full lists of trees and shrubs for hedges, screens and shelter belts are given in Appendix 2, the Tree Directory.)

If garden hedges are to establish quickly and provide a dense screen they will require careful planting and initial maintenance. As the trees or shrubs are planted close together there must be ample supplies of plant food in the soil. If planting at 300mm (1ft) centres, excavate a trench 450mm (1ft 6in) deep and 450mm (1ft 6in) wide and fork well-decomposed manure into the base. The back-fill soil should be of good quality, improved if necessary with compost or slow-release fertilisers. Plant firmly and at the correct height and apply a liberal layer of mulching material. Long thin shoots should be cut back to within two or three buds of the main stem. During dry periods in the first one or two seasons, apply adequate water. As the shoots extend after establishment, keep them pruned back to encourage dense growth at the base of the hedge.

Shelter Belts

In areas of high altitude, and particularly near the

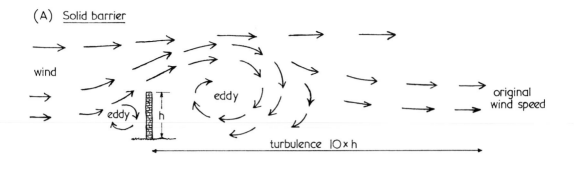

(A) Solid barrier

wind

eddy

eddy h

original
wind speed

turbulence 10 × h

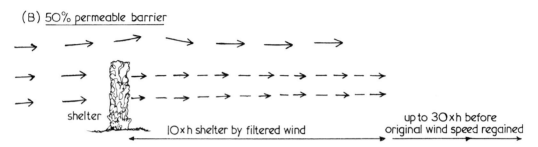

(B) 50% permeable barrier

shelter

10 × h shelter by filtered wind

up to 30 × h before
original wind speed regained

Fig. 22 Effect of solid and permeable barriers on wind

coast, wind can seriously affect both crops and animals and create unpleasant living conditions. Plant barriers in the form of hedges or shelter belts can help reduce this problem and are far more effective than solid fencing or walls. A solid barrier at right-angles to the prevailing wind will, in fact, increase the wind speed to the leeward of the wall by creating intense turbulence. The most effective barrier is one with 50 per cent permeability. This filters the wind and can give very good shelter on the leeward side for a distance of over ten times the height of the barrier, with gradually decreasing shelter for up to thirty times the height of the barrier. This shelter can be very important to many horticultural crops and garden situations. Trees and shrubs not only form effective screens but are cheaper and more acceptable in the landscape than wooden, brick or concrete walls.

For garden situations a hedge will normally provide adequate shelter. The hedge height and thickness can be varied by the selection of species and planting distances. A single row of, say, Escallonia planted at 450mm (1ft 6in) spacings will provide a satisfactory 1m (3ft) high hedge in three years. Closer planting or, better still, a double staggered row of plants will produce an effective screen more quickly.

On a field scale shelter belts are required, with the extra height provided by trees and the low shelter by shrubs. Two or three rows of trees planted at 1·5–2m (5–7ft) spacing between trees and rows will provide adequate shelter for most situations. As the trees mature the low branches may be suppressed and shrub planting on the windward side will be required. The Ministry of Agriculture's Rosewarne Experimental Horticultural Station in Cornwall has carried out extensive trials on a range of trees and shrubs for shelter hedges and trees, and their Station Leaflet No. 2 (3rd edition 1976) gives full details of the results.

11 Legal Rights and Responsibilities

Over the past years successive governments have introduced many statutes which affect trees, and in common law there are many case histories which guide us as to the rights and responsibilities of tree owners and those affected by trees. This chapter only summarises the main provisions, and those with a legal query should always consult a solicitor.

Statute Law

An increasing number of Acts of Parliament have a direct or indirect bearing on trees, and owners should be aware of the following statutes.

Tree protection and felling control

Owing to the increasing pressures on land, a number of laws have been put on the statute books which control felling, help protect our existing tree cover and ensure operator and public safety.

Tree Preservation Orders (TPOs) were originally introduced many years ago but the most recent Acts which set out the procedures and controls are:

1 Town and Country Planning Act 1971, Section 60
2 Town and Country Amenities Act 1974, Section 10
3 Criminal Law Act 1977, Section 28(2)

These Acts empower the local planning authority to protect trees in the interest of amenity. The owner of the tree is not allowed to fell, top, lop or uproot protected trees without the consent of the local planning authority unless the tree is dead, dying or dangerous, or to abate an actionable nuisance. Since these exceptions are arguable, it is always advisable to notify the council of any intended work or, in the case of an emergency, to obtain evidence that the tree was dangerous. The owner of the tree has the right to appeal against a TPO and in the case of a dispute the Department of the Environment acts as arbiter.

Once the Order is confirmed the owner is subject to prosecution if he does fell the tree or destroy its amenity value. The penalties were amended by Section 28(2) of the Criminal Law Act 1977 as follows: on summary conviction a maximum fine of £1,000, or twice the sum which

appears to the court to be the value of the tree, which ever is the greater (see Evaluation of Amenity Trees, p. 96). If the offence is indictable there is no upper limit to the fine, which may be related to any likely profit that could be made by felling the tree(s). This could be important where the unscrupulous developer wishes to build extra houses on a plot of land. All confirmed TPOs are registered in the Local Land Charges Register available at your local authority offices.

The existence of a TPO does not remove the owner's common law responsibilities, and the tree must be maintained at the owner's cost. If permission is given to fell a protected tree, the local planning authority can insist that a replacement tree of an appropriate size and species is planted, again at the owner's expense.

Because of the administrative costs, many local authorities only protect trees where there is a known risk of damage, but any owner or group can request the local authority to issue an order if a tree is considered to be of high amenity value.

The public can also act as watchdogs and inform the local authority if protected trees are under threat.

Trees in conservation areas are additionally protected and anyone proposing to cut down, top or lop *any* tree over 3in (75mm) in trunk diameter is required to give six weeks' notice of his intentions to the local planning authority. This gives the authority an opportunity to make a Tree Preservation Order on the tree(s). If work is carried out without due notice or without the authority's consent, the owner becomes liable to penalties smiliar to those for contravention of a TPO.

Tree owners, those responsible for trees and contractors employed to carry out tree-work operations should, therefore, check with the local planning authority to see whether the trees in question are under a TPO or are growing in a conservation area.

Felling Licences are required in all areas apart from Inner London boroughs when it is proposed to fell more than 825cu ft (23m³) or about 8–10 large trees) of timber in any three month period and when more than 150cu ft (4m³) is to be sold. The licences are issued by the District Office of the Forestry Commission under Section

9 of the Forestry Act 1967. Licences are not required for trees under 3in (75mm) in diameter or for fruit trees or trees in gardens, churchyards and public open spaces.

The main objective of the Felling Licence is to limit and control the volume of timber being felled in any one area, but where there is an amenity interest the Commission will consult with the local planning authority. Although this control regulates large-scale felling, an owner can still fell several large trees every three months. Therefore the public can request the local planning authority to issue a TPO where trees are of high amenity value and there is the likelihood of felling.

Further details of tree protection and felling controls are given in the following publications:

Department of the Environment circular 36/78 (Welsh Office circular 64/78), *Trees and Forestry* (60p from HMSO)
Department of the Environment leaflet *Tree Preservation, a guide to procedure*

Dangerous trees

The local authority has statutory powers to ensure public safety by requiring the owner of a dangerous tree to remove that danger.

The *Local Government (Miscellaneous Provisions) Act 1976*, Sections 23 and 24, enables district councils to take action when asked to do so by the owner or occupier of the land or by a neighbour. If the council considers the tree to be dangerous and the owner fails to make it safe by felling or surgery, the council has the right to carry out the work and recover expenses from the owner.

Under Section 10 of the *Highways (Miscellaneous Provisions) Act 1961* the highway authority has the power to secure the removal of a tree where there is a danger of the tree or part of the tree falling on the highway. Section 134 of the *Highways Act 1959* empowers the highway authority to cut back any vegetation which overhangs the highway.

The Highways Act also states that it is an offence to light a fire within 50ft (15m) of the centre of a made-up carriageway, and if any tree work results in blockage of any part of the highway it is necessary to erect road signs and cones to conform to Chapter 8 of the *Traffic Signs Manual*.

Tree planting and grant aid

The government has through various Acts encouraged tree planting with financial assistance but, to ensure public safety, has also introduced regulations with regard to the planting of trees near highways.

The *Highways Act 1959*, Section 123, states that trees may not be planted within 15ft (5m) of the centre of a made-up carriageway, and that in all cases they should be sited so as not to obstruct the footpath, restrict road users' visibility or obstruct traffic signs and lights.

Grant aid is available from a number of government sources. The *Forestry Commission's* Dedication Scheme (Basis III) offers financial assistance for areas of over 10 hectares (25 acres), and is primarily designed for commercial timber production. Their Small Woods Scheme is designed to encourage planting and maintenance of areas of between ¼ hectare and 10 hectares (0·6–25 acres). Although sound forestry practices are expected, this scheme also takes into account amenity; in lowland, predominantly broadleaf areas preference is given to grant-aiding broadleafed species. Further details of the Forestry Commission's grant-aid scheme are given in their booklet *Advice for Woodland Owners*.

The *Countryside Commission* is empowered, under Section 9 of the Local Government Act 1974, to allow financial assistance for tree planting in the countryside for amenity purposes. Their scheme can also help towards the costs of fencing small woods to encourage natural regeneration, and, in certain circumstances, of tree surgery. Further details of this scheme are available in the Countryside Commission leaflet *Grants for Amenity Planting and Management*. Application forms are obtainable from your county or district council.

The *Nature Conservancy Council* can assist in the establishment and maintenance of nature reserves, and this can include tree planting.

Grant aid for shelter belts that directly benefit agriculture or horticulture is available from the *Ministry of Agriculture, Fisheries and Food*.

The *Department of the Environment* and the *Welsh Office* can offer help in special areas, for example for planting on derelict land or in outstanding conservation areas, special local authority housing schemes or outstanding historic gardens. Details are given in DOE circulars 17/77 and 23/77.

The *Tree Council* has launched a fund-raising scheme and hopes to be able to make money available to grant-aid tree planting and maintenance, especially in areas not covered by the government grants, particularly urban localities.

See Appendix 1, Sources of Advice and Information, for all the relevant addresses.

Plant health regulations

The *Plant Health Act 1967* was introduced in an

attempt to prevent the entry of pests and disease organisms from other countries. The Act is also used on occasions to restrict the spread of existing diseases such as Dutch elm disease. It requires that all live plant material be inspected at the port of entry, and any infected plant may be confiscated and destroyed without recompense.

New regulations are issued from time to time as the need arises; therefore it is advisable to check with the Ministry of Agriculture or the Forestry Commission for the most up-to-date information.

Safety at work
The Health and Safety at Work, etc. Act 1974 covers nearly all employers and employees and is designed to ensure the safety of those at work and the effects of their work on the general public.

Tree work, which involves machinery, handling timber, climbing and working in public areas, presents many dangers to both operator and public. It is the management's responsibility to ensure that staff are properly equipped and trained for the work, and the employees must also act responsibly to ensure safe working conditions.

The Act empowers the Safety Executive staff to inspect working conditions and can require employers to improve their methods or stop work if necessary.

Further details of the Act – *The Act Outlined* – are available from the Health and Safety Commission (see Appendix 1 for address).

Common Law

Over many years various court decisions have given a guide to the rights and responsibilities of both tree owners and those affected by trees. Some examples are mentioned here, but it is always advisable to consult a solicitor if you have a legal query concerning trees.

Ownership of trees
Since the owner of the tree is responsible for it and will have to answer any claims for damages, it is essential to determine who in fact does own the tree. Where a tree is standing inside a defined boundary and there is an owner/occupier, then clearly it is the owner of the land who owns the tree. Difficulties can arise, however, where trees are on or near to boundaries or where there is a tenancy agreement.

Property boundaries may or may not be well defined. The deeds of the property may clarify the position, but in many cases there is no precise measurement. Trees and hedges themselves may form the boundary, and determining ownership can be an involved process.

It is the position of the tree trunk, not the spread of the branches or roots, which determines ownership. If there is a query it is better for it to be settled and agreed before the matter ever comes to litigation, and the services of a chartered surveyor may be required for this. On occasions joint ownership and responsibilities may be agreed. Acts of ownership such as previous maintenance of the hedge or tree may be acceptable as proof of ownership, but on many occasions neighbours will maintain only their own side of a hedge.

If there is a ditch between properties it can be argued that the person who originally dug the ditch would do this to the edge of his property and therefore put the spoil on to his land. If a hedge or trees were then planted in the excavated soil the owner of the ditch would be the owner of the trees.

Tenancy agreements between landlord and tenant should include responsibilities and rights regarding trees. Unfortunately, there are many agreements where trees are not referred to and this can cause problems in the event of any claims, particularly from a third party. It is necessary, therefore, to check the agreement and, if trees are not covered, to ensure that a clause is inserted.

Neighbours' rights
Owners or occupiers of land or property adjoining trees have the right to the air above and the soil beneath their plot. Therefore, they can remove any overhanging branches or invading roots back to the boundary line. The wood thus removed, however, remains the property of the tree owner and the neighbour should not convert the wood, leaves or fruit to useful gain such as firewood, compost or apple pie! He must also be careful not to take more than his 'pound of flesh' and not to trespass on the adjoining land while carrying out the work.

It is always preferable to consult and agree with neighbours, particularly if the branch removal would spoil the shape, amenity and safety of the tree. Some local planning authorities also notify neighbouring landowners of the existence of Tree Preservation Orders so as to prevent the unnecessary mutilation of trees.

Tree roots have given rise to many claims for damages to adjoining property. On shrinkable clay soils, and particularly in long dry periods, large vigorous trees can extract huge volumes of water from the soil, causing foundation settlement and damage. In such instances, where there are neighbouring trees in the proximity, many people have tried to obtain compensation from the tree owners.

If there are roots under the damaged building and these can be positively identified as coming from the neighbouring tree(s), there is little defence, but it is always worth checking to see whether any other site factors could have influenced the soil moisture content.

Few realise that if large trees are felled the soil could swell considerably when wet, and this could result in far more damage.

The main risk is from large vigorous trees such as poplars and willows on shrinkable clay soils, and owners should avoid planting such species or ensure that they are planted at least one and a half times the ultimate height of the tree away from buildings, drains etc. When building new properties closer to existing trees than one and a half times their height, the solution is to construct stronger and deeper foundations which will not be damaged by soil settlement. British Standard *Trees in Relation to Construction* is in the course of preparation and will give further details concerning trees near buildings.

On soils other than clay and for smaller species of tree there is not so much of a problem, but always give thought to the ultimate size and spread of the tree and its roots.

Right of light

If neighbours have enjoyed light to their property for an uninterrupted period of at least twenty years then they could have a claim against any person who plants a large tree close to their property and thereby blocks that light.

It will be difficult for neighbours to claim any right to light if small trees grow slowly and cast increasing shade over many years or if no part of the tree's branches or roots actually encroaches on to their land. However, if large, fast-growing trees are planted only a few feet from a person's window I would suggest that his light has been dramatically reduced and he could request that those trees be removed.

Dangerous trees

Trees can grow to very large proportions and if they are situated near public areas the owner should ensure safety for both public and property by regularly inspecting his trees and correcting any faults by surgery or, if necessary, felling.

No tree is 'safe', but in any claim for damages it will be necessary to prove that the owner was negligent. Could or should the tree owner have foreseen the danger and removed or repaired the tree before the accident occurred? If it can be proved that the tree was showing obvious symptoms of distress then it is likely that the owner will be liable.

Determining what is an obvious symptom is not always easy. Clearly if the tree is dead or there are large dead branches, then the owner should fell the tree or have the dead wood removed. Again, large open cavities or rots should be obvious, as should the presence of large fungal growths on the roots, trunk or branches, or major root damage. However, some internal rots and weaknesses may be obvious only to the trained eye, and then confirmed only by detailed examination (see Chapter 6, Care of Existing Trees). If the owner of the tree is a local authority, a large estate or a botanic garden, then the court will expect a higher degree of knowledge of tree danger symptoms than it would from, say, an old-age pensioner in a semi-detached cottage.

Regular tree inspections by a qualified person and immediate action in the event of finding dangerous trees are the best ways of safeguarding the public. Anyone making tree inspections should be fully trained in the recognition of danger symptoms and able to spot the abnormal. Casual observations from ground level will not always be sufficient. Climbing inspections may be necessary to investigate an old pruning scar, a suspect fork or just a woodpecker hole. Test-boring with an auger or increment borer will help the trained inspector, and there is also a decay-detection meter available in the USA. This 'Shigometer' is now under trial at the Forestry Commission's research station at Alice Holt, and should prove to be a very useful aid.

However, to inspect every tree regularly at least once a year, and preferably once in summer and once in winter, is not always feasible or financially practicable for the owner. If it is possible to remove only the obviously dangerous trees, it is absolutely essential that adequate insurance be taken out to cover the others if and when negligence is proven. Simply to erect a notice stating that a tree is dangerous does not remove the owner's liability in the event of damage. In public areas the owner must protect the public by erecting a physical barrier to prevent access under or near to the tree.

Poisonous species also come under the heading of dangerous trees, and there have been many claims for damage to farm stock and children. If any part of the poisonous plant can be reached without the animal or child having to enter the property or lean over the fence, then the owner could be liable. Yew and Rhododendron are two examples of trees which often give rise to claims,

56 An obviously dying and dangerous tree left
standing by a public highway

and plants such as Laburnum and Daphne should not be planted in children's playgrounds.

Evaluation of Amenity Trees

It is often necessary to put a value on a tree. This may be required in order to assess the monetary worth of a tree when a Tree Preservation Order has been contravened, or as a means of calculating the role of trees in a landscape, particularly when planning future development.

Any system must be standardised, disciplined and as objective as possible. One such system, devised by Mr D. R. Helliwell and known as the 'Helliwell System', was adopted by the Tree Council and has been used as a means of evaluation in court. The system has six standard factors, and each factor is considered in turn and awarded a score between 1 and 4. All the scores are multiplied together to arrive at a value. A seventh factor can also be used if there is some really special factor such as important historic association or extreme rarity.

When assessing the value for each factor, the following guidelines are used:

The Helliwell System

| FACTOR | POINTS | | | |
	1	2	3	4
1 Size of tree	small	medium	large	very large
2 Useful life expectancy	10-20 yrs	20-40 yrs	40-100 yrs	100+ yrs
3 Importance of position in landscape	little	some	considerable	great
4 Presence of other trees	many	some	few	none
5 Relation to the setting	barely suitable	fairly suitable	very suitable	especially suitable
6 Form	poor	fair	good	especially good
7 Special factors	none	one	two	three

Factor 1: Size of tree
Score 1 – small: 3–10m² (30–100sq ft) (height×mean crown diameter)
Score 2 – medium: 10–50m² (100–500sq ft)
Score 3 – large: 50–200m² (500–2,000sq ft)
Score 4– very large: over 200m² (2,000sq ft)

Factor 2: Useful life expectancy
Assessed in years of safe, good condition for its situation: i.e., a tree near a road needs to be in a very good condition, but a tree well away from the public could be retained and provide a useful amenity even if rotten in the trunk.

Factor 3: Importance of positon in landscape
Score 1 – little importance: trees in rural areas, back gardens or in a group of trees or woodland
Score 2 – some importance: individual roadside trees in residential areas, public parks or gardens
Score 3 – considerable importance: prominent individual trees in well-frequented places

Score 4 – great importance: trees which are of crucial importance to well-known places

Factor 4: Presence of other trees
Score 1 – many: more than 30 per cent of the visual area covered by trees and at least ten trees in the area concerned
Score 2 – some: more than 10 per cent of the visual area covered by trees and at least four trees present
Score 3 – few: less than 10 per cent of the visual area covered by trees and at least one other tree present
Score 4 – none: no other trees present

The visual area is not always easy to define, but in residential areas it is normally quite obvious between roads, houses etc.

Factor 5: Relation to the setting
Again, sometimes difficult to be purely objective, but the tree should look in keeping with the area and not likely to cause problems. For example, a

small-growing tree in a large open space would perhaps score only 1; likewise a very large dense tree too close to a house and causing shade and other problems.

Factor 6: Form
Consideration should be given to the shape and balance of the tree and its relation to the typical form for the species. A badly mutilated, damaged or lopped tree might well score only 1, but a beautifully shaped tree would score high.

Factor 7: Special factors
Used only very occasionally, when the tree has an important historic association or is of a particularly rare species or form. A tree in a formal avenue would warrant a special score because if it were removed the visual effect would be spoilt; similarly, a tree hiding an ugly view from a focal point would score high. One special factor would score 2, two special factors score 3, and so on.

Using this system to assess the value of a free-standing oak tree on a village green, the following might be the result:

> Factor 1: score 4
> Factor 2: score 3
> Factor 3: score 3
> Factor 4: score 3
> Factor 5: score 4

Factor 6: score 2
no special factors
Total $= 4 \times 3 \times 3 \times 3 \times 4 \times 2 = 864$ points

An old apple tree in a rear garden might produce the following:

> Factor 1: score 2
> Factor 2: score 1
> Factor 3: score 1
> Factor 4: score 2
> Factor 5: score 3
> Factor 6: score 2
> no special factors
> Total $= 2 \times 1 \times 1 \times 2 \times 3 \times 2 = 24$ points

When this system was published by the Tree Council in 1974 it was suggested that if it were necessary to put a monetary value on a tree, then each point should be worth £1.00. When the system was used in a court in 1975 the value was raised to £1.25 per point to allow for inflation.

It can be seen, therefore, that this system permits considerable value to be placed on good trees. In disputes each side would of course award low or high values to suit its own case, but if these were averaged a fair value could be assessed.

For further details, see the Tree Council leaflet *An Evaluation Method for Amenity Trees*. The Helliwell System was first published in the Arboricultural Associaton's *Journal*, Vol. 1 No. 5 (1967).

12 Tree Disorders

Trees, even those growing in natural conditions, are subject to damage from a great range of disorders, and when they are growing in artificial areas such as towns or amid intensive agriculture, there are many additional damaging agents. Some disorders will kill directly, others weaken or disfigure the tree and render it prone to secondary problems.

Luckily few of the 'natural' disorders are fatal and trees only succumb to a combination of attacks. The few which are fatal normally attack and kill only one particular species or related trees and so long as there is a good distribution of species the overall tree cover will not be unduly affected. Dutch elm disease, which is one such killer, has destroyed the majority of elms in the southern half of the country. The widespread publicity given to this one disease has generated a great deal of interest in amenity tree problems and now with more research, money and public sympathy available the remaining tree cover could benefit in the future.

Undoubtedly the most serious threat to trees is man; with the ever-increasing development and re-development of towns, roads and agriculture, more and more trees are being affected. Direct damage by man, i.e. unnecessary felling, lopping and general abuse of trees, is serious enough but can be controlled to some extent by legislation. More worrying is the indirect damage caused by pollution, apathy or ignorance. The aggressive fatal form of Dutch elm disease could not have crossed the Atlantic without the help of man. To avoid further losses all landowners and all those responsible for trees must use the lessons of Dutch elm disease to safeguard our landscape for the future.

Trees can be damaged by a vast range of agencies and a full study of this subject would require a separate volume. This chapter summarises the main problems, identifies examples of the main disorders and suggests methods of prevention or control.

It must be remembered that a disorder attacking one part of the tree could severely affect another part and the whole tree could be threatened: a leaf disease, for example, will reduce or prevent the process of photosynthesis, and therefore the entire tree will be starved of energy. Similarly, if the roots are severed when foundations are laid for a new building, the leaves will not receive sufficient water and nutrients and will soon wilt or die.

Diseases

Diseases caused by fungi, bacteria and viruses are very common. Some of the fungi and bacteria are classed as saprophytic, living on dead tissue and helping in the breakdown of humus into available plant nutrients. Others have a symbiotic relationship with plants, each deriving some benefits from the other. *Rhizobium* bacteria help leguminous plants and trees to obtain nitrates from the soil, and fungal *Mychorriza* live on tree roots but make soil nutrients available to the tree. Other fungi, bacteria and viruses feed on living plant tissue and are classed as parasites. These parasites cause plant diseases, the most serious being those dealt with in the following pages. Additional information on identification and treatment can be obtained from the Forestry Commission and Ministry of Agriculture leaflets listed.

Leaf diseases

Oak powdery mildew
This leaf mildew, caused by the fungus *Microsphaera alphitoides*, is common on small trees and the young shoots of mature trees. The upper leaf surface is covered by a white powdery growth and this reduces the leaf's ability to photosynthesise. Therefore in severe attacks the tree is weakened but seldom killed. In nurseries and on young trees effective control can be achieved by spraying with benomyl or a sulphur fungicide.

Tar spot on sycamore
Black, raised tar-like spots are produced on the upper surface of the leaf by the fungus *Rhytisma acerinum*. The disease is unsightly but, except in severe attacks when the whole leaf is covered, the tree will not be unduly affected. In gardens, the best control is to rake up and burn all infected leaves.

Virus diseases of trees
Although much study has been made of virus

diseases of crops and fruit trees, as yet there is little detailed knowledge of virus and virus-like diseases of ornamental trees.

The viruses invade and damage the tissues of the leaf and other parts of the plant. Typical symptoms are yellowing, mottling or curling of the foliage and general lack of vigour in the shoots.

Viruses can be spread by seed and vegetative forms of propagation, by aphids and other insects, by root-infecting fungi, natural root grafts and pruning tools. Prevention is the only cure. Virus-free propagation material is used in nurseries, particularly with fruit trees and trees of the rose family. The control of insect vectors and the sterilising of tools after cutting known diseased trees will also help.

(See Forestry Commission Arboricultural Leaflet No. 4, *Virus and Virus-like Diseases of Trees*.)

Other common leaf diseases include needle rusts of pines and other conifers, Keithia disease of western red cedar, grey moulds (Botrytis) in nurseries and needle cast of pines.

Diseases of shoots and branches

Anthracnose of willows
The fungus *Marsonina saliciola* causes open cankers on the young shoots of willows. This disease is common following a cold wet spring. It can cause shoot death and general weakening of the tree. On a small scale, prune out and burn diseased wood or spray with a fungicide, Morestan, at bud-break.

There is also a London plane anthracnose.

Coral spot
A common fungus, *Nectria cinnabarina*, causes orange/coral spots on dead twigs. This can cause problems in nurseries where pruned shoots can be attacked and the fungus can spread from the dead stumps into the main stem. Trees in the maple family are particularly susceptible.

Strict hygiene is the best means of preventing the disease becoming widespread. All prunings should be cleared and burnt before autumn when the spores will spread. In nurseries and fruit orchards a fungicidal tree paint is used to protect cut surfaces.

Coryneum cardinale
This is a fungus attacking Cupressus trees, causing cankers on the branches and trunks. All infected wood should be removed and burnt.

Bacterial cankers
Poplar canker, caused by the bacterium *Aplanobacterium populi*, is commonly seen; not only does it disfigure the tree, but branches are weakened and can die and break off in winds. A great number of poplar species and cultivars are resistant and therefore only these should be selected for planting.

Other bacterial cankers affect plums, Prunus and ash trees.

Vascular wilt diseases

Fire blight
Fire blight is a serious disease of fruit trees, trees and shrubs in the rose family caused by the bacterium *Erwinia amylovora*. It is particularly serious in apple- and pear-growing regions as it infects the vascular system and shoots and flowers are affected, which means that there will be no fruit. The disease also attacks a variety of ornamental trees and shrubs such as Cotoneaster, thorns and Pyracantha.

In fruit-growing areas of the country the disease should be notified to the Ministry of

59 *Coryneum cardinale* fungus on Leyland cypress

60 Poplar bacterial canker

Agriculture, and diseased plants should be removed and burned.

Watermark disease of cricket bat willow

This disease, caused by the bacterium *Erwinia salicis*, can be serious in the bat willow production areas. The disease blocks the vascular system, causing leaves to wilt and redden, and the whole branch dies. If infected branches are cut through, brown staining can be seen in the sapwood area. The only control is to fell and burn infected trees. The Watermark Disease (Local Authority) Order 1974 (Statutory Instrument No. 768) empowers the following local authorities to insist that diseased trees are felled and burned: the county councils of Bedfordshire, Cambridgeshire, Essex, Hertfordshire, Suffolk and Norfolk and the London boroughs of Barking, Enfield, Havering, Newham and Redbridge.

(See Forestry Commission leaflet No. 20, *Watermark Disease of the Cricket Bat Willow*.)

Dutch elm disease, Ceratocystis ulmi

This is another example of a fungus disease which blocks the vascular system in the sapwood of the tree, so that the leaves receive no water and soon wilt and die. Once into the sapstream the fungus can be spread throughout the tree and death follows very quickly. This is one of the few diseases which is almost certain to be fatal, and its effect on the elm population in the southern half of the British Isles is well known.

The disease can spread from one tree to the next via root suckers, but more commonly the fungus is distributed by a small beetle. The beetles, *Scolytus scolytus* and *Scolytus multistriatus*, use the diseased tree as a host for breeding. After mating the female beetle burrows under the bark and lays a number of eggs. The following spring the larvae pupate, and new adults emerge from the diseased tree in early summer. These new young adults now spend a period of time feeding externally on neighbouring healthy elm trees, and in so doing unwittingly transmit the disease. The beetles can fly a mile or two, but the process is accelerated by the movement of diseased timber, carrying the beetle, to other parts of the country for use. A vicious circle rapidly develops, because as the fungus affects more trees, so it provides more habitats for the beetle.

In most of the southern half of England the disease is now so widespread that there is no control. A few isolated pockets of elms are worth protecting, and it is encouraging to see authorities such as East Sussex County Council and Brighton Borough Council carrying out

61 Beech bark disease and beech scale insects

62 Large bracket fungus, *Piptoporus betulinus*, and woodpecker hole, indicating internal rotting

strict hygiene felling programmes. On a county scale this is difficult, but in towns like Brighton a vigilant parks department and the help of the public are resulting in a very limited spread of the disease.

Further north the spread of the disease from the south is controlled by the Dutch Elm Disease (Restriction on Movement) Order 1977 (SI 1977 No. 1075). This order prohibits the movement of elm timber into certain areas unless the bark is removed. The areas covered by this order are listed in the Dutch Elm Disease (Local Authorities) Order (SI 1977 No. 1074). Details are available from your local Conservator of Forest (see p. 114).

Injecting the trees with fungicides has had some success as a preventive measure, but the injections need to be repeated regularly and can be expensive.

(See Forestry Commission leaflet No. 54, *The Control of Dutch Elm Disease*, 1974, and Forest Record No. 115, *Dutch Elm Disease*, 1977.)

Bark diseases

Beech bark disease

The most serious disease affecting our woodland beech trees, this is caused by a fungus, *Nectria coccinea*, and aided by a scale insect, *Cryptococcus fagi* (see p. 106). The insect lives on the bark and causes direct injury and general weakening of the tree. The fungus gains entry through the damage caused by the insect. Larger strips of bark will die with the vertical spread of the fungus. The vascular system is infected and the leaves turn yellow. Severely attacked trees can be killed within a few years, and the trunks will be liable to wind-break.

In woodlands, localised severe attacks should be controlled by felling infected trees. On specimen trees a tar-oil winter wash applied with a pressure sprayer will help control the scale insect.

(See Forestry Commission Forest Record No. 96, *Beech Bark Disease*.)

Sooty bark disease of sycamore

This disease of sycamore, caused by the fungus *Cryptostroma corticale*, was first observed in the late 1940s in north-east London; although a number

of trees were killed, the disease died out, with only minor outbreaks in the 1950s. However, in 1976, following a particularly dry summer, a severe outbreak spread the range of the disease to most areas of southern England.

The fungus forms a brownish-black dry sooty layer of minute spores just under the bark, which dies and flakes off. The spores are spread in the wind and will infect other trees, mainly through open wounds. The vascular system of the tree is affected and the leaves wilt. The disease is far more serious following hot dry summers; normal cool wet conditions will act as a natural control.

Infected and killed trees should be removed or they will soon become dangerous. Although felling will release many of the spores, a number will be destroyed by burning the wood. All cut surfaces should be properly painted. Plant a wide range of species, but avoid the planting of sycamore altogether in known diseased localities.

(See Forestry Commission Arboricultural Leaflet No. 3, *Sooty Bark Disease of Sycamore*.)

Wood rots

A great number of fungus diseases attack and destroy the wood of tree trunks, branches and roots. They do not always directly kill the tree, but the entire structure is weakened and far more liable to wind-blow or breakage of trunk and branches.

Fomes annosus causes one of the most serious diseases in forestry, as it attacks mainly conifers. The fungus first gains entry through freshly cut stumps of felled trees and spreads to neighbouring trees by the roots. The only effective treatment is to treat all stumps with a 20 per cent solution of urea. This will prevent the disease becoming established. On pines a biological control is used by applying a spore suspension of *Peniophora gigantea*. (See Forestry Commission leaflet No. 5, *Fomes annosus*.)

Ganoderma applanatum is commonly found attacking the trunks of a range of hardwood trees, while other diseases such as *Inonotus hispidus* on ash and *Piptoporus betulinus* on birch are mainly specific to one genus of tree.

Most of the wood-rotting fungi produce large bracket-like fruiting bodies on the trunks, branches or roots, and these are obvious indicators of internal rots. These brackets should be removed and burnt to prevent the spread of the disease to other trees. Since the spores gain entry through exposed wounds, all pruning cuts etc. should be properly treated.

Root diseases

Honey fungus

This disease is one of the most common causes of the death of trees and shrubs, and if the tree is not directly killed, it is severely weakened and easily blown over or attacked by secondary problems.

103

63 Honey fungus toadstools in autumn

64 Black bootlace-like rhizomorphs of honey fungus;
roots rotten and tree blown over

The fungus *Armillariella mellea* invades the roots and stumps of trees, resulting in decay. Clumps of honey-coloured toadstools appear in the autumn at soil level or on the base of the trunk. If the bark is removed at the base of the trunk a creamy-white mass of fungal growth can be seen. The fungus also develops tough, black, bootlace-like growths called rhizomorphs. These rhizomorphs can spread under the bark or through the soil and invade surrounding trees and shrubs. Once the disease is established the leaves turn yellow and twigs die back. There is little control, but infected trees, stumps and as much of the root system as possible should be removed and burned.

If planting on known diseased soil it is best to plant trees of lower susceptibility, i.e. beech, ash, holly, larch, thorns, sweet gums, oak, Douglas and silver firs, rhus, false acacia, yews and limes.

(See Forestry Commission Arboricultural Leaflet No. 2, *Honey Fungus*.)

Phytophthora root rot

This disease is often confused with honey fungus but despite its name it kills rather than rots the roots of trees and shrubs. Unlike honey fungus it does not produce toadstools or rhizomorphs. It is, however, a serious disease affecting nursery soils, particularly in wet conditions. Trees such as horse and sweet chestnut, Rhododendrons, Lawson cypress, beech, apples, yew, lime and poplar are particularly susceptible.

The disease can be identified by dead bark on the roots and lower portion of the stem, death of leaves and die-back of twigs and branches. Nurseries with infected soils are growing trees in containers to prevent soil contact. When planting susceptible species, avoid creating situations where water could collect around the stem, as this will encourage the disease.

Insect Pests

Insects and insect-like creatures can directly attack and damage trees and are frequently the carriers or vectors of diseases. Few, luckily, reach epidemic proportions in this country, except perhaps in monocultures in some forestry plantations.

Most insects undergo a number of changes in their life cycle from egg through larva and pupa to adult. It is the larval and adult stages which cause the damage, but sometimes the best form of control is to attack the more dormant egg or pupa.

As with diseases, any part of the tree is open to attack. Descriptions of some of the more common and important insect pests are given in the following pages.

Leaf, bud and fruit pests

Sawflies

The pine sawfly, *Diprion pini*, is a common pest attacking the foliage of pine species. The adult female lays eggs on the needles and the resulting caterpillars eat the foliage. In the case of the apple sawfly, *Hoplocampa testudinea*, the caterpillars burrow into young developing apples and in severe outbreaks destroy the crop. (See MAFF Advisory Leaflet No. 13, *Apple Sawfly*.)

Moths

The winter moths, *Operophtera brumata* and *O. fagata*, again cause damage to fruit trees by eating holes in the leaves, flower buds and young fruitlets. (See MAFF Advisory Leaflet No. 11, *Winter Moths*.)

The pine beauty moth has always been a common but economically unimportant pest on Scots pine, but is now a serious threat to plantations of lodge pole pine in Scotland. The caterpillar can, in severe outbreaks, completely defoliate young trees, with fatal results. Major insecticide spraying programmes are being carried out.

Aphids

Greenflies are a very common garden pest and many will attack and cause damage to trees and shrubs. They are also often responsible for the transmission of virus diseases. The insects feed on the leaves and cause distortion and eventual death. In severe outbreaks spraying with insecticides can be very effective. (See Forestry Commission Forest Records No. 84, *Winter Temperatures and Survival of Green Spruce Aphid*, 1972, and No. 104, *Towards Integrated Control of Tree Aphids*, 1975.)

Leaf miners

A number of insects burrow into the leaf and cause damage. The holly leaf miner, *Phytomyza ilicis*, is very common on ornamental and hedging hollies, but is not often serious enough to cause real damage. Removal and burning of the unsightly leaves is the best control.

Red spider mites

A number of red spider mites attack and damage foliage. The fruit tree red spider mite, *Panonychus ulmi*, sucks the sap of the leaves and prevents the process of photosynthesis. (See MAFF Advisory Leaflet No. 10, *Fruit Tree Red Spider Mite*.)

Twig and shoot pests

Adelges

A number of species of *Adelges* cause damage to conifers, particularly spruce trees. The insects attack the needles and pineapple-shaped galls develop on the shoots. This pest can become a problem on nursery trees, where control will be necessary. (See Forestry Commission leaflets No. 2, *Adelges cooleyi*, and No. 7, *Adelgids attacking Spruce and other Conifers.*)

Woolly aphid

The whooly aphid, *Eriosoma lanigerum*, is a common pest on fruit and garden trees but can be controlled by spraying with insecticides. (See MAFF Advisory Leaflet No. 187, *Woolly Aphid.*)

Weevils and beetles

A number of weevils and beetles cause direct damage to trees and often act as disease vectors, as in the case of Dutch elm disease.

The large pine weevil, *Hylobius abietis*, is a common and serious pest on pines, particularly in nurseries and young plantations, as are the black pine beetles, *Hylastes species*. (See Forestry Commission leaflet No. 58, *The Large Pine Weevil and Black Pine Beetles.*)

Branch and trunk pests

Scale insects

The females of these insects live under a protective scale-like covering on the branches and shoots of trees. By feeding on the sap they can, in severe outbreaks, cause severe damage.

The felted beech coccus, *Cryptococcus fagi*, is also involved in the damage caused by beech bark disease (see p. 102). Winter washes with tar oil will normally control this pest on a garden scale.

Bark-boring insects

Many beetles use trees as their nesting sites and the female beetle burrows through the bark and lays a series of eggs. When the eggs hatch the larvae feed on the tree and emerge through the bark as adults. This can cause direct damage to and death of the bark and conductive tissue; moreover, as the adults then migrate to other trees, they can spread harmful disease organisms, as in the case of Dutch elm disease.

Wood-boring insects

The goat moth, *Cossus cossus*, although not common, can cause severe damage to individual trees. The caterpillar, up to 75mm (3in) long, tunnels into the wood of the trunk, as does the leopard moth, *Zeuzera aesculi*.

65 Severe damage caused by the grey squirrel

66 Deer fraying damaging bark

Root pests

Chafer grubs

The grubs of the chafer beetle *Melolontha melolontha* and other chafers feed on the roots of trees, causing, in severe outbreaks, death of the roots. (See MAFF Advisory Leaflet No. 235, *Chafer Grubs.*)

Swift moths

The ghost swift moth, *Hepialus humuli*, and the garden swift moth, *H. lupulina*, cause damage through their white caterpillars, which feed on the roots of trees, shrubs and other plants. The caterpillars tunnel into the pith region of the roots, which become hollow. These pests can be a serious problem in nurseries and young plantations. (See MAFF Advisory Leaflet No. 160, *Swift Moths.*)

Black Vine Weevil

This pest is becoming a problem in nurseries. The adult weevil feeds on the leaves, eating out semi-circular segments from the leaf edge. The main damage, however, is caused by the larvae, which feed on the fine roots, causing wilting of the foliage and stunted growth. (See MAFF Advisory leaflet No. 57, *Black Vine Weevil.*)

Animals and Birds

One of the most useful functions of trees is to provide habitat and food for wildlife, but on occasions the animals or birds can become so numerous that they do serious harm and control or preventive measures become necessary. Farm animals also can cause severe damage if trees are not adequately protected.

Mice and voles

Small rodents can cause serious difficulties in the nursery by eating seed and roots and damaging propagation material. In large numbers they can also affect small trees in plantations. Control by trapping or poisoning will reduce the problem in the nursery.

Squirrels

The red squirrel is a very attractive and relatively harmless creature which should be protected and

encouraged in our countryside. However, the grey squirrel is a much more aggressive and damaging pest and must be controlled.

The grey squirrel will eat the bark of a number of tree species, particularly that of young trees and the softer bark on the upper branches of large trees. Once the branches have been girdled the section above will die and the tree will become weakened and disfigured.

Unfortunately, there is no effective guard or fence that can be erected against a small climbing animal like the squirrel. The only method of control is to kill by trapping, shooting or poisoning. Removing the nests or dreys can also reduce the population. (See Forestry Commission leaflet No. 56, *Grey Squirrel Control.*)

Rabbits

The advent of myxomatosis eradicated most of the wild rabbits in this country, but such are their infamous powers of breeding that in many places their numbers are now so large that severe damage is being done and control is required. The harm is caused by the rabbits eating the young shoots or bark of trees. This is a real problem in hard winters, and it is necessary either to protect the trees or to control the rabbit population by shooting or trapping.

When planting trees in areas where rabbits are numerous it is normal to protect the trees by the use of plastic or wire guards (see pls. 16 and 17). In plantations it is often necessary to erect rabbit-proof fencing around the whole site.

(See Forestry Commission leaflet No. 67, *Rabbit Management in Woodlands.*)

Deer

Wild deer are very attractive animals, but they can cause considerable damage to young trees and to the lower branches of larger trees. Direct eating of the shoots is serious enough, but deer also injure trees when they rub the down off their antlers ('fraying') against the branches.

The overall numbers of deer are controlled, but local damage in nurseries and plantations can be prevented by the erection of fencing or by using animal repellants.

(See Forestry Commission leaflet No. 52, *The Fallow Deer*; Forest Record No. 99, *The Roe Deer*; and leaflet No. 73, *Chemical Repellants.*)

Farm animals

All grazing and browsing animals can severely damage trees. Young trees are particularly vulnerable, but even large trees can be damaged by bark stripping and breakage of branches. Free-roaming sheep, particularly in upland areas, will prevent natural regeneration by eating the young seedlings.

If trees are standing inside grazing areas,

adequate fencing or guards will be required to prevent damage (see pls. 3, 18 and 19).

Birds
The majority of birds do little damage, and their presence should be encouraged to control insects; furthermore, many of them are legally protected. However, with some species – particularly in large numbers – serious problems can be caused and control is necessary.

Finches can be a menace in fruit orchards, destroying the fruiting crop by eating or picking off the flower buds. Prevention by netting the trees or erecting bird-scarers is commonplace in fruit-growing areas.

Starlings are a source of annoyance in many areas when they roost in trees in large flocks. They normally feed in the open countryside and return to their roosting sites at night. In towns this can be a nuisance because of their noise and droppings, with sometimes thousands of birds in one large tree. (See Forestry Commission leaflet No. 69, *Starling Roost Dispersal.*)

Pigeons seem to favour the developing flower buds of ash trees. This can cause loss of flowers and consequently fruit on attacked trees, but does not appear to affect the leaves. In severe attacks one remedy is to lace the trees with black thread, which disturbs the birds. This is only necessary on important feature trees, as the cost of protecting a large tree could be very high.

Damage by Other Plants

Trees are normally the dominant form of vegetation and can outgrow smaller plants. However, young transplants can be suppressed by vigorous weed growth before they are established, and some climbing plants can cause damage or hide problems.

Some epiphytic plants (i.e. those growing on trees but not of parasitic habit), such as lichens, mosses and ferns, are common on tree trunks and branches. This can 'disfigure' the trees, particularly in mild and moist areas of the country, but control is not usually necessary.

In this country semi-parasitic plants (i.e. those living on and taking nutrients from the host tree) are also found. Mistletoe is one such semi-parasite, but it does little damage and is often encouraged on fruit and lime trees because of its seasonal market value.

Weeds
Weeds are the most serious plant problem, particularly in nurseries and around recently planted small trees. The annual growth rate of the weeds is often much faster than that of the trees, which are consequently suppressed. Weed control or eradication is therefore necessary.

With newly planted trees, it is best to keep the area around the stem clear of weed growth by mulching, the use of 'Treespats' (see pl. 26) or mechanical or chemical control. There is a great variety of chemicals available for killing or controlling weeds. These are generally called *herbicides*.

Climbing plants
Some climbing plants can provide very attractive features and can very quickly cover and hide old stumps or other unsightly features. Some, however, can climb into living trees and, if permitted to develop, can suppress the branches and leaves of the tree, cause actual damage by girdling the twigs and branches and hide faults in the trunks.

Honeysuckle climbs by spiralling around the stem and on young trees and branches the tree can be severely distorted by the resultant constriction.

Old man's beard or clematis is a fast-growing native climbing plant, particularly on chalk soils. If left it will soon cover small trees and bushes in hedgerows.

Ivy is often blamed for killing trees, and some people think the plant is parasitic on the host. This is not the case. The small root-like growths which attach the ivy to the tree are only for anchorage and do not extract any nutrients from the tree. However, there are two problems with this plant. Firstly, the ivy can grow into the crown of the tree and, being evergreen, can suppress the lower branches and twigs. The second problem is that dense ivy growth on the trunks can hide faults and weaknesses such as cavities and split forks, and will limit proper tree inspections. However, ivy does provide habitats for a variety of wildlife and is thus a very useful plant in woodlands.

In general, therefore, climbing plants should not be allowed to become dominant in any tree; they can be controlled by cutting off at ground level.

(See Forestry Commission Forest Record No. 102, *Three Forest Climbers: Ivy, Old Man's Beard and Honeysuckle.*)

Adverse Weather

Being a comparatively small group of islands, the British Isles experience many climatic variations. These provide a great range of growing conditions and therefore a wealth of trees and

shrubs can be successfully grown. If trees are carefully selected to suit the prevailing climatic conditions most will survive, but some extremes of our climate can have an adverse effect.

As can be seen from Chapter 3, Tree Growth, the environment of the tree is one of the major factors influencing growth. The processes of growth, water and nutrient absorption and the manufacture and conversion of energy will only function properly in certain conditions. Extreme cold or heat, lack of or excess water and exposure will all affect the tree. Damage can also be expected from wind, hail and lightning. Many of these problems can be avoided by the proper selection of trees (see Appendix 2, Tree Directory).

Frost

Most trees and shrubs from the temperate regions can tolerate low temperatures and are protected by being deciduous or by bearing needle-like or tough leaves which are less liable to damage. The main risk arises where half-hardy trees are selected for planting in what are normally the milder parts of the country, or planted in other areas against south-facing walls. In the event of severe frost considerable damage, including scorching or death of leaves and shoots, can be expected. Another problem is the occurrence of late frosts in May and June, when the young foliage and shoots of even hardy trees can be killed.

On a large scale nothing can be done to prevent damage, but small trees and wall shrubs can be individually protected with sacking or by covering with straw. Known frost-tender subjects (those listed under Mild Climate in the Tree Directory) should be planted where there is least risk of frost damage, i.e. under the shelter of larger trees and close to south-facing walls. Avoid planting in frost pockets such as low-lying areas.

Wind

Free-standing healthy trees can normally withstand even the most severe gales, but when surrounding shelter is removed, for example in woodland thinning, or if trees are weakened by root damage or stem rots, then the whole tree can blow over. This is known as wind-throw. In permanently exposed sites a tree's shape will be influenced by the prevailing winds.

Sometimes the main trunk or branches will break in high winds. Important trees can be protected by bracing (see Chapter 7, Tree Pruning and Surgery), but in woodlands care should be taken to avoid clear felling or over-thinning of areas which are providing shelter.

Salt-laden winds near the coast can also cause scorching and death of leaves, particularly in the summer. In dry soil conditions the wind will carry particles of grit which again can cause damage.

Drought

The lack of available soil water will cause the delicate root hairs to die and therefore the leaves will wilt and eventually die. This is why we must regularly irrigate recently planted trees, but even established trees can suffer in prolonged dry periods. Many large shallow-rooted beech trees died as a result of the 1976 drought.

Flooding

Temporary flooding with unpolluted water does little damage but prolonged flooding or water containing toxic substances can soon kill or weaken trees. Tree roots can also be exposed and damaged through the erosion caused by running water.

Sun and shade

Some trees are light-demanding and will grow towards the available light; others are shade-tolerant and will grow successfully under the canopy of higher trees. Again, selection is important to ensure proper growth (see Tree Directory).

Some trees can be damaged by sun-scorch or crack. This can occur when trees are heavily thinned or pruned and the bark is suddenly exposed to the sun.

Snow, ice and hail

The weight of heavy snow or ice on branches can cause breakage. This is a particularly serious problem with the heavy horizontal branches of spreading conifers such as cedars. Bracing can reduce the likelihood of damage.

Hail, particularly in summer, can cause severe damage to foliage and fruit. Little can be done to prevent this, but ensure that the trees are properly maintained and healthy, as the loss of foliage could exaggerate other problems.

Lightning

Trees are natural lightning conductors, especially the tall-growing species such as redwoods and other conifers. The rapid expansion of the sap into steam as a result of the extreme temperatures can cause complete breakage of the branch or trunk, or severe cracking. It is possible to erect lightning conductors in trees, but few would warrant this

68 Lightning crack invaded by fungus and insects and
later by woodpeckers feeding on the insects

69 Fire – one of the greatest threats to trees in
   plantations, hedges and woodlands

expense. If trees are damaged they should be repaired as soon as possible to prevent the entry of harmful organisms.

Damage by Man

In most parts of the world man is the tree's worst enemy. As has been mentioned earlier man has, over the centuries, used the land on which trees grow for his own needs and through greed or ignorance has dramatically reduced the tree cover. Much publicity has been given to this topic and happily many more people are now conscious of the need to protect existing trees and to plant more for the future.

Increased legislation and tighter planning controls are reducing the loss of trees on development sites and in the countryside, and more and more government departments and local authorities are employing professional arboricultural staff. In addition, members of the public can do much to help by refraining from felling or lopping trees in gardens or by planting replacement trees.

Vandalism is a major social problem costing many millions of pounds every year. In some areas it is not practical to plant trees as they will invariably be pulled up or broken. Involving children in tree-planting activities and using woodlands for educational projects can help instil a greater awareness of the importance of trees (see pl. 10). Parents too can help prevent vandalism by setting an example and showing an interest in the environment. It is important to realise that even the carving of initials on tree trunks can give rise to the entry of harmful organisms.

Fire is one of the most damaging of hazards facing trees, particularly in dry conditions and in young plantations. The general public can reduce this risk to the countryside by not lighting fires in dry periods, extinguishing cigarettes carefully and not leaving behind combustible litter or glass.

Stubble and straw burning is now a necessary and important aid to arable farming. It allows for quick post-harvest cultivation, discourages weed infestation and reduces the risk of straw-borne diseases. However, great care must be taken when burning in order to avoid damage to surrounding hedgerows, trees, neighbouring property and wildlife. The national Farmers' Union has issued a very useful *Straw and Stubble Burning Code* which details how and when burning should be carried out.

In woodland areas free advice on fire prevention and control can be sought from the chief officer or firemaster of the local fire brigade.

Use of Chemicals

A great range of chemicals is used for pest and disease control and for controlling or killing vegetation. Many are very effective and comparatively harmless, but others are highly toxic and can kill or damage plants, animals and humans. It is essential, therefore, always to read the instructions carefully and never to allow children or animals access to such chemicals. The Ministry of Agriculture, under the Agricultural Chemicals Approval Scheme, produces an annual list of approved products and their uses for farmers and growers. This lists approved insecticides, fungicides and herbicides and other chemicals; the introductory chapter gives advice on their safe use.

Appendix 1: Sources of Advice and Information

This practical guide to tree planting and care is intended to give basic help and instruction to landowners and those responsible for trees, but because of the complexity of the subject and the inherent dangers of some of the work further professional advice and information may be required.

Advice and Grant Aid

Several government departments and agencies provide advice on various aspects of forestry and arboriculture and offer grant aid for specific purposes.

Forestry Commission

For forestry and woods over ¼ hectare (0·6 acre) on private land producing utilisable timber; also general arboricultural advice through their research station at Alice Holt in conjunction with the Department of the Environment.

Headquarters:	The Forestry Commission, 231 Corstorphine Road, Edinburgh EH12 7AT (Telephone: 031-334 0303)
London Office:	The Forestry Commission, 25 Savile Row, London W1X 2AY (Telephone: 01-734 4251)
Research Stations:	The Forestry Commission, Forest Research Station, Alice Holt Lodge, Wrecclesham, Farnham, Surrey GU10 4LH (Telephone: 042-04 2255)
	The Forestry Commission, Northern Research Station, Bush Estate, Roslin, Midlothian EH25 9SY (Telephone: 031-445 2176)

Conservancy Offices, England:

North-west:	Dee Hills Park, Chester CH3 5AT (Telephone: 0244 24006)
North-east:	1A Grosvenor Terrace, York YO3 7BD (Telephone: 090 420221)
East:	Block D, Government Buildings, Brooklands Avenue, Cambridge CB2 2DY (Telephone: 0223 58911)
South-east:	The Queen's House, Lyndhurst, Hants SO4 7NH (Telephone: 042128 2801)
South-west:	Flowers Hill, Brislington, Bristol BS4 5JY (Telephone: 0272 713471)

Conservancy Offices, Scotland:

North:	21 Church Street, Inverness IV1 1EL (Telephone: 0463 32811)
South:	Greystone Park, 55157 Moffat Road, Dumfries DG1 1NP (Telephone: 0387 2425)
East:	6 Queen's Gate, Aberdeen AB9 2NQ (Telephone: 0224 33361)
West:	Portcullis House, 21 India Street, Glasgow G2 4PL (Telephone: 041248 3931)

Conservancy Offices, Wales:

North:	Victoria House, Victoria Terrace, Aberystwyth, Dyfed SY23 2DA (Telephone: 0970 612367)
South:	Churchill House, Churchill Way, Cardiff CF1 4TU (Telephone: 0222 40661)

Forestry Commission publications (Sectional List No. 31) are available from HMSO, 49 High Holborn, London WC1V 6HB, or from Alice Holt Research Station.

Countryside Commission
For amenity planting in the countryside. Detailed advice for grant aid through local county or district council.

England: John Dower House,
                  Crescent Place,
                  Cheltenham,
                  Glos GL50 3RA
                  (Telephone: 0242 21381)

Wales;   8 Broad Street,
                  Newtown,
                  Powys SY16 2LU
                  (Telephone: 0686 26799)

Countryside Commission for Scotland
Battleby,
Redgorton,
Perth PH1 3EW
(Telephone: 0738 27921)

Directorate of Ancient Monuments and Historic Buildings, Department of the Environment
25 Savile Row,
London W1V 2BT
(Telephone: 01-734 6010)

Grant aid for planting in gardens or land of outstanding historical interest and for planting to preserve or enhance an outstanding conservation area.

Ministry of Agriculture, Fisheries and Food (Agricultural Development and Advisory Service)
Great Westminster House,
Horseferry Road,
London SW1P 2AE
(Telephone: 01-216 6286)

Grant aid for shelter belts and advisory service for commercial establishments.

Nature Conservancy Council
20 Belgrave Square,
London SW1X 8PY
(Telephone: 01-235 3241)

Grant aid for planting in areas managed for nature conservation.

Professional Advice and Organisations

A number of professional bodies issue lists of registered or approved consultants and/or contractors for the range of forestry/arboricultural activities, and provide other services to their members through journals,

conferences, local meetings etc.

Arboricultural Association
Brokerswood House,
Brokerswood,
Nr Westbury,
Wilts BA13 4EH
(Telephone: 0373 822238)

Issues *Directory of Consultants and Contractors* for arboricultural advice and work, and a range of publications (see p. 118).

Association of Professional Foresters of Great Britain
Brokerswood House,
Brokerswood,
Nr Westbury,
Wilts BA13 4EH
(Telephone: 0373 822238)

Forestry management and contractors.

British Association of Landscape Industries
The Coach House,
St Ives, Bingley,
West Yorks BD16 1AT
(Telephone: 09766 2006)

Landscape contractors for construction and maintenance of hard and soft landscape features.

Institute of Foresters of Great Britain
6 Rutland Square,
Edinburgh EH1 2AV
(Telephone: 031-229 4010)

Forestry advice and management.

Landscape Institute
12 Carlton House Terrace,
London SW1Y 5AH
(Telephone: 01-839 4044)

Landscape architects and planners.

Scottish Woodland Owners' Association Ltd
6 Chester Street,
Edinburgh EH3 7RD
(Telephone: 031-226 3475)

Advice to members on forestry and woodland management.

Timber Growers' Organisation Ltd
c/o National Agricultural Centre,
Kenilworth,
Warwickshire CU8 2LG
(Telephone: 0203 21559)

Advice to members on forestry and woodland management.

Royal Forestry Society of England, Wales and Northern Ireland
102 High Street,
Tring,
Herts HP23 4AN
(Telephone: 0442 82 2028)

Royal Scottish Forestry Society
18 Abercromby Place,
Edinburgh EH1 2BU
(Telephone: 031-557 1017)

Horticultural Trades Association
18 Westcote Road,
Reading,
Berks RG3 2DE
(Telephone: 0734 581371)

National Farmers' Union
Agriculture House,
Knightsbridge,
London SW1X 7NJ
(Telephone: 01-235 5077)

Royal Horticultural Society
Vincent Square,
London SW1P 2PE
(Telephone: 01-834 4333)

Voluntary Organisations

Individuals or corporate bodies may wish to become actively involved with local amenity groups or voluntary organisations. Each of the organisation headquarters in the following list will provide details of their activities in your particular area.

Arboricultural Association
Brokerswood House,
Brokerswood,
Nr Westbury,
Wilts BA13 4EH
(Telephone: 0373 822238)

Eight regional branches.

Civic Trust
17 Carlton House Terrace,
London SW1Y 5AW
(Telephone: 01-930 0914)

Concerned with the protection and environment of towns, cities and villages; 1,300 local societies on its register.

Civic Trust for the North-east
34/35 Saddler Street,

Durham
(Telephone: 0385 61182)

Civic Trust for the North-west
56 Oxford Street,
Manchester M1 6EU
(Telephone: 061-236 7464)

Civic Trust for Wales/Treftadaeth Cymru
46 Cardiff Road,
Llandaff, Cardiff
(Telephone: 0222 552388)

Council for the Protection of Rural England
4 Hobart Place,
London SW1W 0HY
(Telephone: 01-235 4771)

Over forty branches and county committees to protect rural scenery and amenities of country towns and villages.

Council for the Protection of Rural Wales/Cymdeithas Doigelu Harddwch Cymru
Meifod,
Powys SY22 6DA
(Telephone: 093 884 383)

Men of the Trees
Crawley Down,
Crawley,
Sussex
(Telephone: 0342 12536)

Branches in seven counties to encourage the planting and preservation of trees.

British Trust for Conservation Volunteers (The National Conservation Corps)
c/o Zoological Gardens,
Regents Park,
London NW1 4RY
(Telephone: 01-722 7112)

Working parties of volunteers for conservation tasks which have public benefit.

The Tree Council

35 Belgrave Square,
London SW1X 8QN
(Telephone: 01-235 8854)

The Tree Council provides a forum for the various organisations concerned with trees and land use and ownership, to help educate the public in the appreciation of trees and to encourage tree planting in the landscape and proper maintenance of trees. It provides a limited fund for financial assistance for tree planting and maintenance, particularly in areas not covered by other grant aid schemes, and organises 'National Tree Week' in the autumn of each year to attract greater publicity to its objectives.

Education and Training

Short training courses in the various skills of forestry and arboriculture are available at a number of centres, and full educational career courses are offered at craft, diploma and degree levels.

Short training courses
Local Government Training Board,
8 Arndale Centre,
Luton,
Beds LU1 2TS
(Telephone: 0582 21111)

Co-ordinates and prepares instructor manuals for training courses for local authority staffs.

Honey Bros (Sales) Ltd,
New Pond Road,
Peasmarsh,
Guildford,
Surrey
(Telephone: 0483 61362)
in conjunction with
Peter Bridgeman & Associates,
20 Wood Street,
Ash Vale,
Nr Aldershot,
Hants GU12 5JG
(Telephone: 0252 27903)

Offer range of short courses in specific skills of arboriculture, particularly tree surgery safety, either at Guildford or at the employer's own premises.

Educational courses
Craft and diploma level courses are available at a number of educational establishments.

Merrist Wood Agricultural College,
Worplesdon,
Guildford,
Surrey GU3 3PE
(Telephone: 048 631 2424)

Offers a comprehensive range of courses including 10-week course on Tree Surgery for Craftsmen, 1-year course for National Certificate in Horticulture (Arboriculture), and 3-year course for Ordinary National Diploma in Arboriculture.

Other courses are available at:

Askham Bryan College of Agriculture and Horticulture,
Askham Bryan,
York UO2 3PR
(Telephone: 0904 66232)

Cheshire College of Agriculture,
Reaseheath,
Nantwich,
Cheshire
(Telephone: 0270 65131)

Capel Manor Institute of Horticulture,
Bullsmoor Lane,
Waltham Cross,
Herts EN1 4RW
(Telephone: 0992 38480)

There are no specific *degree courses* available in arboriculture, but BSc and BA, MSc and doctoral degrees in forestry and allied subjects are available at Oxford, Bangor, Aberdeen and Edinburgh universities.

Safety

The Forestry Safety Council
Forestry Commission,
231 Corstorphine Road,
Edinburgh EH12 7AT
(Telephone: 031-334 0303)

Produces a range of free safety guides for specific skills of forestry and arboricultural work.

The Health and Safety Commission
Health and Safety Executive,
Baynards House,
1 Chepstow Place,
London W2 4TF
(Telephone: 01-229 3456)

Issues a number of leaflets explaining the scope of the Health and Safety at Work, etc. Act 1974.

Publications

A vast range of leaflets, booklets and books is available on various aspects of forestry and arboriculture.

Leaflets and booklets
The main organisations producing free or low-priced leaflets and booklets are as follows.

The *Forestry Commission's* Sectional List 31 lists the various publications issued; a catalogue of publications is also available. The publications may be obtained through HMSO, 49 High

Holborn, London, from the regional government bookshops and from the Commission's research station at Alice Holt.

The *Tree Council* produces a range of leaflets on *Tree Surveys, Evaluation of Amenity Trees, Tree Planting and Community Woodlands, Tree Planting and Maintenance* and *Tree Care*.

The *Arboricultural Association*'s booklets cover the following topics:

Tree Preservation Orders
Trees – A Guide to Pruning
The Care of Trees on Development Sites
Trees – Site Preparation and Planting
A Tree for Every Site
Trees and the Law
Tree Notes for Amenity Societies
Trees for Small Gardens

The *Nature Conservancy Council* publishes a free booklet, *Tree Planting and Wildlife Conservation*.

BBC Publications, 35 Marylebone High Street, London W1 publish *The Nationwide Book of British Trees*.

The Recommendations and Codes of Practice of the *British Standards Institution*, 2 Park Street, London W1A 2BS (telephone: 01-629 9000), include the following:

BS3882 *Recommendations and Classification for Top Soil*
BS3936 *Nursery Stock*:
        Part 1 *Trees and Shrubs*
        Part 2 *Roses*
        Part 3 *Fruit*
        Part 4 *Forest Trees*
        Part 5 *Poplars and Willows for Timber*
BS3975 *Glossary for Landscape Work*
BS3998 *Recommendations for Tree Work*
BS4043 *Recommendations for Transplanting Semi-Mature Trees*
BS4156 *Peat*
BS4428 *General Landscape Operations*
BS5236 *Recommendations for the Cultivation and Planting of Trees in the Advanced Nursery Stock Category*
BS   *Trees in Relation to Construction* (in course of preparation)

Books

Over the past three centuries there has been an ever-increasing number of books published on tree topics. Reference has already been made to John Evelyn's famous *Sylva*, published in 1664. John Loudon's *Arboretum of Fructicetum Britannicum* (1842) recorded all the hardy trees known in mid-nineteenth-century Britain.

The seven volumes of Elwes & Henry's *Trees of Great Britain and Ireland* were published only in a limited edition (1906–13) and original sets now cost hundreds of pounds. Luckily, a facsimile published in 1969 by SR Publishers with the Royal Forestry Society is available.

In 1914 W. J. Bean published his two volumes *Trees and Shrubs Hardy in the British Isles*; the eighth edition fills four volumes and is the authoritative work.

A. D. C. Le Sueur's *The Care and Repair of Ornamental Trees* set standards of tree care and maintenance when published in 1934. Since the 1950s we have seen a great range of books published. Some are specific to a single genus, while larger 'coffee-table' glossies attempt to cover every aspect of the romance, science and practice of tree care. A brief selection of some of the notable works indicates the range available:

Bloom, Adrian, *Conifers for your Garden* (Floraprint, 1972)
Bridgeman, P. H., *Tree Surgery* (David & Charles, 1976)
Brown, G. E., *The Pruning of Trees, Shrubs and Conifers* (Faber, 1972)
Caborn, J. M., *Shelter Belts and Windbreaks* (Faber, 1965)
Clapham, A. R., *Oxford Book of Trees* (OUP, 1975)
Edlin, H. L., *Guide to Tree Planting and Cultivation* (Collins, 1970)
—— *Trees, Woods and Man* (Collins, 1974)
Hillier, H., *Hillier's Manual of Trees and Shrubs* (David & Charles, 1977)
James, N. D. G., *The Arboriculturalist's Companion* (Blackwell, 1972)
Johnson, Hugh, *International Book of Trees* (Mitchell Beazley, 1973)
Johnson, W. T., *Insects that Feed on Trees and Shrubs* (Cornell University Press, 1976)
Kozlowski, Theodore T., *Growth and Development of Trees* (2 vols, Academic Press, 1971)
Lamb, Kelly and Bowbrick, *Nursery Stock Manual* (Grower Books, 1975)
Lancaster, Roy, *Trees for your Garden* (Floraprint, 1974)
Miles, Roger, *Forestry in the English Landscape* (Faber, 1967)
Mitchell, Alan, *A Field Guide to the Trees of Britain and Northern Europe* (Collins, 1974)
Peace, T. R., *Pathology of Trees and Shrubs* (out of print but still the standard reference work)
Rackham, Oliver, *Trees and Woodlands in the British Landscape* (Dent, 1976)
Rehder, A., *Manual of Cultivated Trees and Shrubs* (Macmillan, 1940)
Wilks, J. H., *Trees of the British Isles in History and Legend* (Muller, 1972)

Appendix 2: Tree Directory

M. J. Whitehead, ND Arb, Kew Dip (Hort)

Contents

The following lists are aimed to assist in the selection of trees for various sites and purposes. Availability and cost will depend on type of propagation, seasonal availability of seed, traditions and marketing trends in the production of plants, and whether the trees are uncommon or rare. For example, the "Golden oak", *Quercus robur* 'Concordia', is fairly well known in the horticultural trade, but it is a very rare tree owing to the unavailability of plant material for propagation, the tree's slow rate of growth, and lack of promotion within the trade and demand by the public. Rare plants and uncommon or disused cultivars are included in the lists in the hope of promoting more demand and thus increasing their use. Shrubby trees have also been included, some of which may take time to attain tree-like stature, while others will require the removal of lower branches and the selection of sturdy stems to enable them eventually to form trunk-like proportions.

Size

Deciduous (native and naturalised trees)

Large

Acer platanoides	*Quercus cerris*
Acer pseudoplatanus	*Quercus ilex*
Aesculus hippocastanum	*Quercus petraea*
Alnus glutinosa	*Quercus robur*
Betula pendula	*Quercus rubra*
Betula pubescens	*Salix alba*
Carpinus betulus	*Salix fragilis*
Castanea sativa	*Tilia cordata*
Fagus sylvatica	*Tilia* × *europaea*
Fraxinus excelsior	*Tilia platyphyllos*
Juglans regia	*Ulmus glabra*
Populus alba	*Ulmus procera*
Populus canescens	(elm varieties)
Populus nigra	
(hybrid poplars)	

Medium

Acer campestre	*Pyrus communis*
Populus tremula	*Sorbus domestica*
Prunus avium	*Sorbus torminalis*
Prunus padus	

Small (including shrubby native trees)

Amelanchier lamarckii	*Prunus spinosa*
Corylus avellana	*Rhamnus cathartica*
Crataegus monogyna	*Salix caprea*
Crataegus oxyacantha	*Salix pentandra*
Euonymus europaeus	*Salix triandra*
Hippophae rhamnoides	*Sambucus nigra*
Malus sylvestris	*Sorbus aria*
Prunus cerasus	*Sorbus aucuparia*
Prunus domestica	*Viburnum opulus*

Evergreen (native)

Large

Ilex aquifolium	
Pinus sylvestris	
Taxus baccata	

Small

Arbutus unedo	
Buxus sempervirens	
Juniperus communis	

Shape

Rounded

Large

Acer platanoides
Acer pseudoplantanus
Aesculus hippocastanum
Carpinus betulus
Fagus sylvatica
Nothofagus procera

Quercus ilex
Quercus robur
Pinus radiata
Platanus × hispanica
Tilia cordata
Zelkova carpinifolia

Medium

Acer campestre
Acer cappadocicum
Acer opalus
Carpinus betulus 'Globosa'
Celtis australis
Diospyros virginiana
Euodia danellii
Fraxinus ornus

Ilex aquifolium
Koelreuteria paniculata
Ligustrum lucidum
Phellodendron chinensis
Pinus pinea
Prunus avium
Pyrus communis
Sorbus domestica
Zelkova sinica

Small

Acer palmatum
Acer japonicum
Amelanchier lamarckii
Cornus florida
Cornus mas .
Crataegus monogyna 'Inermis'
Gleditsia triacanthos 'Elegantissima'

Liquidambar orientalis
Magnolia kobus
Malus sylvestris
Morus nigra
Prunus cerasus
Robinia pseudoacacia 'Bessoniana'
Robinia pseudoacacia 'Inermis'

Irregular outline

Alnus glutinosa
Fraxinus excelsior
Gleditsia triacanthos
Hippophae rhamnoides
Nothofagus antarctica

Prunus laurocerasus
Robinia hispida
Robinia pseudoacacia
Robinia viscosa
Salix fragilis
Ulmus procera

Conical

Alnus cordata
(conifers)
Corylus colurna
Eucalyptus dalrympleana
Eucryphia × nymansensis 'Nymansay'
Ilex opaca
Laurus nobilis

Magnolia salicifolia
Nyssa sylvatica
Ostrya virginiana
Oxydendrum arboreum
Pyrus calleryana 'Chanticleer'
Sassafras albidum

Fastigiate (upright)

Large

Acer pseudoplatanus 'Erectum'
Calocedrus decurrens
Cedrus atlantica 'Fastigiata'
Chamaecyparis lawsoniana 'Erecta'
Chamaecyparis lawsoniana 'Robusta Glauca'
Chamaecyparis lawsoniana 'Wisselii'
Chamaecyparis lawsoniana 'Witzeliana'
Cryptomeria japonica 'Lobbii'
× *Cupressocyparis leylandii*

Cupressus macrocarpa 'Donard Gold'
Cupressus sempervirens
Fagus sylvatica 'Dawyck'
Ginkgo biloba 'Fastigiata'
Populus alba 'Pyramidalis'
Populus nigra 'Italica'
Quercus robur 'Fastigiata'
Robinia pseudoacacia 'Fastigiata'
Thuja plicata 'Fastigiata'

Ulmus augustifolia var *cornubensis*
Ulmus glabra 'Exoniensis'

Ulmus × *sarniensis*
Zelkova carpinifolia

Medium

Abies alba 'Pyramidalis'
Acer × *lobelii*
Acer platanoides 'Columnare'
Acer rubrum 'Scanlon'
Acer saccharinum 'Pyramidalis'
Acer saccharum 'Monumentale'
Aesculus hippocastanum 'Pyramidalis'
Alnus glutinosa 'Pyramidalis'
Betula pendula 'Fastigiata'
Carpinus betulus 'Fastigiata'
Castanea sativa 'Pyramidalis'
Chamaecyparis lawsoniana 'Allumii'
Chamaecyparis lawsoniana 'Columnaris'
Chamaecyparis lawsoniana 'Fraseri'
Chamaecyparis lawsoniana 'Kilmacurragh'
Chamaecyparis lawsoniana 'Pottenii'
Cupressus abramsiana
Cupressus glabra 'Pyramidalis'

Cupressus goveniana
Ilex aquifolium 'Green Pillar'
Juniperus chinensis 'Aurea'
Larix decidua 'Fastigiata'
Liriodendron tulipifera 'Fastigiata'
Picea abies 'Pyramidata'
Pinus sylvestris 'Fastigiata'
Populus simonii 'Fastigiata'
Populus tremula 'Fastigiata'
Quercus castaneifolia 'Green Spire'
Quercus petraea 'Columnaris'
Taxodium ascendens 'Nutans'
Taxus baccata 'Fastigiata'
Thuja occidentalis 'Fastigiata'
Tilia americana 'Fastigiata'
Tilia cordata 'Swedish Upright'
Tilia platyphyllos 'Fastigiata'

Small

Alnus viridis
Aralia chinensis 'Pyramidalis'
Austrocedrus chiliensis
Betula pendula 'Obelisk'
Buxus sempervirens 'Pyramidalis'
Carpinus betulus 'Columnaris'
Cephalotaxus harringtonia 'Fastigiata'
Chamaecyparis lawsoniana 'Ellwoodii'
Chamaecyparis lawsoniana 'Fletcheri'
Crataegus monogyna 'Stricta'
Fagus sylvatica 'Cockleshell'
Juniperus chinensis 'Keteleerii'
Juniperus chinensis 'Pyramidalis'
Juniperus communis 'Hibernica'
Juniperus scopulorum 'Erecta Glauca'
Juniperus scopulorum 'Spring Bank'
Juniperus virginiana 'Burkii'
Juniperus virginiana 'Skyrocket'
Koelreuteria paniculata 'Fastigiata'
Laburnum alpinum 'Pyramidale'
Laburnum anagyroides 'Erect'
Laurus nobilis var *augustifolia*
Magnolia grandiflora 'Fastigiata'
Malus × *micromalus*
Malus prunifolia 'Fastigiata'
Malus tschonoskii
Malus 'Van Eseltine'
Morus alba 'Fastigiata'
Prunus 'Amanogowa'

Prunus dulcis 'Erecta'
Prunus × *hillieri* 'Spire'
Prunus lusitanica 'Myrtifolia'
Prunus padus 'Stricta'
Prunus 'Pandora'
Prunus sargentiana 'Rancho'
Prunus × *schmittii*
Prunus simonii
Prunus 'Taizanfukun'
Prunus 'Umineko'
Ptelea trifoliata 'Fastigiata'
Pyrus communis 'Beech Hill'
Quercus robur 'Fastigiata Purpurea'
Rhamnus frangula 'Fastigiata'
Sambucus nigra 'Pyramidalis'
Sorbus aria 'Lutescens'
Sorbus aucuparia 'Fastigiata'
Sorbus commixta
Sorbus 'Joseph Rock'
Sorbus meinichii
Sorbus meliosmifolia
Sorbus scopulina
Sorbus 'Sheerwater Seedling'
Sorbus × *thuringiaca* 'Fastigiata'
Taxus baccata 'Aureomarginata'
Taxus baccata 'Standishii'
Ulmus × *hollandica*
Ulmus × *hollandica* 'Wredei'
Ulmus × *sarniensis* 'Dicksonii'

Horizontal (spreading)

Acer capillipes
Acer davidii
Acer tataricum
Aesculus parviflora
Cercidiphyllum japonicum
Cercis siliquastrum

(conifers and taxads – many)
Cornus alternifolia
Cornus controversa
Cornus florida
Cornus mas
Cornus nuttallii

122

Cotoneaster × *watereri*
Hamamelis japonica var *arborea*
Laburnum anagyroides

Northofagus antarctica
Prunus 'Tai Haku'

Pendulous (weeping)

Large

Betula pendula
Cedrus atlantica 'Glauca Pendula'
Cedrus atlantica 'Pendula'
Cedrus deodara
Chamaecyparis lawsoniana 'Intertexta'
Chamaecyparis nootkatensis 'Pendula'
Fagus sylvatica 'Miltoniensis'
Fagus sylvatica 'Pendula'
Fraxinus augustifolia 'Pendula'
Fraxinus excelsior 'Diversifolia Pendula'
Fraxinus excelsior 'Pendula'
Fraxinus excelsior 'Wentworthii'

Larix decidua 'Pendula'
Picea abies 'Inversa'
Picea omorika 'Pendula'
Picea smithiana
Picea spinulosa
Pseudotsuga menziesii 'Pendula'
Salix babylonica
Salix × *chrysocoma*
Salix 'Elegantissima'
Salix 'Sepulcralis'
Tilia petiolaris
Ulmus glabra 'Pendula'

Medium

Abies alba 'Pendula'
Acer saccharinum 'Pendulum'
Alnus incana 'Pendula'
Betula pendula 'Dalecarlica'
Betula pendula 'Purple Splendour'
Betula pendula 'Tristis'
Cedrus deodara 'Aurea Pendula'
Chamaecyparis lawsoniana 'Pendula'
Cupressus macrocarpa 'Pendula'
Fagus sylvatica 'Aurea Pendula'
Ginkgo biloba 'Pendula'
Ilex aquifolium 'Pendula'
Juniperus recurva var *coxii*
Larix kaempferi 'Pendula'
Picea brewerana
Pinus strobus 'Pendula'

Prunus serotina 'Pendula'
Quercus cerris 'Pendula'
Quercus palustris 'Pendula'
Quercus pyrenaica 'Pendula'
Quercus robur 'Pendula'
Salis babylonica 'Annularis'
Salix × *blanda*
Salix × *erythroflexuosa*
Salix matsudana 'Pendula'
Sequoiadendron giganteum 'Pendulum'
Taxodium distichum 'Pendens'
Taxus baccata 'Dovastoniana'
Tsuga canadensis 'Green Mantle'
Ulmus americana 'Pendula'
Zelkova crenata 'Pendula'

Small

Acer negundo 'Pendula'
Acer palmatum 'Dissectum'
Betula pendula 'Youngii'
Buxus sempervirens 'Pendula'
Caragana arborescens 'Pendula'
Carpinus betulus 'Pendula'
Cornus florida 'Pendula'
Corylus avellana 'Pendula'
Cotinus coggyria 'Pendula'
Cotoneaster multiflorus
Cotoneaster salicifolius
Crataegus monogyna 'Pendula'
Dacrydium franklinii
Fitzroya cupressoides
Genista aetnensis
Gleditsia triacanthus 'Bujoti'
Ilex aquifolium 'Argenteomarginata Pendula'
Juglans regia 'Pendula'
Juniperus rigida
Juniperus virginiana 'Pendula'
Laburnum alpinum 'Pendulum'
Laburnum anagyroides 'Pendulum'

Malus 'Echtermeyer'
Malus 'Elise Rathke'
Malus prunifolia 'Pendula'
Malus sieboldii
Morus alba 'Pendula'
Parrotia persica 'Pendula'
Picea abies 'Cranstonii'
Picea pungens 'Pendula'
Populus tremula 'Pendula'
Populus tremuloides 'Pendula'
Prunus avium 'Pendula'
Prunus cerasifera 'Pendula'
Prunus 'Hillings Weeping'
Prunus 'Kiku-shidare Sakura'
Prunus mahaleb 'Pendula'
Prunus mume 'Pendula'
Prunus persica 'Crimson Cascade'
Prunus persica 'Windle Weeping'
Prunus subhirtella 'Pendula Rubra'
Prunus × *yedoensis* 'Shirdare Yoshino'
Pyrus salicifolia 'Pendula'
Salix caprea 'Pendula'

Salix purpurea 'Pendula'
Sambucus nigra 'Pendula'
Sophora japonica 'Pendula'
Sorbus aria 'Pendula'
Sorbus aucuparia 'Pendula'
Sorbus folgneria 'Pendula'

Syringa pekinensis 'Pendula'
Thuja occidentalis 'Pendula'
Tsuga canadensis 'Pendula'
Ulmus glabra 'Camperdownii'
Ulmus × *hollandica* 'Smithii'

Architectural (unusual or bold shape or form)

Abies pinsapo
Aralia chinensis
Araucaria araucana
Brachyglottis repanda
Cedrus libani
Cordyline australis
Cunninghamia lanceolata
Hamamelis japonica var *arborea*

Kalopanax pictus var *maximowiczi*
Picea brewerana
Pinus montezumae
Pseudopanax crassifolius
Sequoiadendron giganteum 'Pendulum'
Taxodium distichum
Trachycarpus fortunei

Ornamental Features

Bark

Abies procera
Abies squamata
Acer capillipes
Acer davidii
Acer griseum
Acer grosseri
Acer hersii
Acer papilio
Acer pensylvanicum
Arbutus andrachne
Arbutus × *andrachnoides*
Arbutus menziesii
Betula (many)
Carya ovata
Castanea sativa
Celtis laevigata
Clethera barbinervis
Clethera delavayi
Cornus kousa
Cryptomeria japonica
Cupressus forbesii
Dipelta floribunda
Eucalyptus (most)
Fagus sylvatica
Ficus carica
Juniperus deppeana var *pachyphlaea*
Lagerstroemia indica

Lyonothamnus floribundus var *aspenifolius*
Myrtus apiculata
Ostrya japonica
Parrotia persica
Phellodendron (most)
Pinus bungeana
Pinus densiflora var *umbraculifera*
Pinus gerardiana
Pinus patula
Pinus pinaster
Pinus ponderosa
Pinus sylvestris
Platanus (all)
Populus canescens
Populus tremuloides
Prunus dawyckensis
Prunus maakii
Prunus × *schmittii*
Prunus serrula
Quercus suber
Quercus variabilis
Salix × *chrysocoma*
Sequoia sempervirens
Sequoiadendron giganteum
Taxus baccata
Zelkova carpinifolia
Zelkova verschaffeltii

Twigs

Contorted

Corylus avellana 'Contorta'
Crataegus mongyna 'Flexuosa'
Robinia pseudoacacia 'Tortuosa'

Salix × *erythroflexuosa*
Salix matsudana 'Tortuosa'

Blackish-purple

Malus 'Eleyi'

Salix 'Black Knight'

124

Scarlet, reddish and maroon

Acer capillipes
Acer palmatum 'Senkaki'
Acer pensylvanicum 'Erythrocladum'
Arbutus andrachne

Arbutus menziesii
Salix alba 'Chermesina'
Tilia platyphyllos 'Rubra'

Orange, gold and yellow

Alnus incana 'Aurea'
Fraxinus excelsior 'Aurea'
Fraxinus excelsior 'Jaspidea'
Salix alba 'Vitalina'

Salix × chrysocoma
Tilia × euchlora
Tilia platyphyllos 'Aurea'

Glaucous, bluish and white

Acer negundo var *violaceum*
Eucalyptus niphophila
Populus alba

Pyrus salicifolia 'Pendula'
Salix acutifolia
Salix daphnoides

Broadleaf evergreen foliage (including shrubby and semi-hardy trees)

Acacia (many)
Acer hookeri
Acer laevigatum
Acer sempervirens
Acer paxii
Acer wardii
Acradenia franliniae
Anopteris glandulosus
Arbutus (all)
Arctostaphylos manzanita
Aristotelia serrata
Atherosperma moschatum
Azara (all)
Berberis insignis
Brachyglottis repanda
Buddleia asiatica
Camellia cuspidata
Camellia reticulata
Castanopsis cuspidata
Chrysolepis chrysophylla
Ceanothus arboreus
Cercocarpus ledifolius
Cinnamomum camphora
Citherarexylum spicatum
Clethra arborea
Cleyera fortunei
Cordyline australis
Cornus capitata
Cornus oblonga
Cotoneaster (various)
Crinodendron patagua
Daphnephyllum macropodum
Distylium racemosa
Drimys winteri
Elaeagnus macrophylla
Embothrium coccineum
Erica arborea
Eriobotrya japonica
Escallonia revoluta
Eucalyptus (all)
Eucryphia (most)

Euonymus myrianthus
Fremontodendron californicum
Garrya elliptica
Gevuina avellana
Gordonia lasianthus
Griselinia littoralis
Hakea sericea
Heteromeles arbutifolia
Hoheria augustifolia
Hoheria populnea
Hoheria sexstylosa
Ilex (all)
Itea ilicifolia
Laurelia serrata
Laurus azorica
Laurus nobilis
Leptospermum scoparium
Ligustrum (most)
Lindera megaphylla
Lithocarpus (all)
Lomatia ferruginea
Lyonothamnus floribundus var *asplenifolius*
Machilius ichangensis
Magnolia (various)
Mahonia acanthifolia
Manglietia insignis
Maytenus boaria
Metrosideros lucida
Michelia doltsopa
Myoporum laetum
Myrica californica
Myrica cerasifera
Myrtus (all)
Neolitsia sericea
Nerium oleander
Notelaea excelsa
Nothofagus (various)
Olea europaea
Olearia arborescens
Osmanthus yunnanensis
Persea borbonia

Peumus boldus
Phillyrea (all)
Photinia (various)
Pittosporum tenuifolium
Pomaderris apetala
Prostranthera ovalifolia
Prunus ilicifolia
Prunus laurocerasus
Prunus lusitanica
Prunus lyonii
Pseudopanax ferox
Pyracantha atalantioides
Quercus (various)
Quillaia saponaria
Reevsia thyrsoidea
Rhamnus alaterna
Rhododendron arboreum

Rhodoleia championii
Sapindus murkorossi
Schima wallichii
Schinus molle
Sophora tetraptera
Stranvaesia davidiana
Sycopsis sinensis
Telopea truncata
Ternstromia gymnanthera
Trachycarpus fortunei
Trochodendron aralioides
Umbellularia californica
Villaresia mucronata
Wienmania racemosa
Xylosma japonica
Yucca brevifolia

Leaf flush colour

Acer (many)
Aesculus neglecta 'Erythroblastos'
Carpinus turczaninowii
Cercidiphyllum japonicum
Fagus (all)
Larix (all)
Neolitsia sericea

Photinia (many)
Quercus alba
Quercus rubra
Salix × chrysocoma
Taxodium (all)
Zelkova sinica

Persistent deciduous leaves (marcescent)

Acer (few)
Carpinus (most – when cut as a hedge)

Fagus (most – when cut as a hedge)
Quercus (few)

Aromatic foliage

Atherosperma moschatum
Cercidiphyllum (autumn)
Clerodendrum (all)
Cinnomomum
(conifers – most)
Eucalyptus (all)
Euodia (few)
Juglans (all)
Laurus (all)
Lindera (all)
Myrica (all)
Myrtus (most)

Parabenzoin
Persea borbonia
Phellodendron (all)
Populus (basalm types)
Ptelea trifoliata
Rhus (most)
Salix (few)
Sambucus
Sassafras
Umbellularia
Vitex agnus-castus
Zanthoxylum (all)

Large bold foliage

Acer macrophyllum
Aesculus (all)
Ailanthus altissima
Aralia (all)
Broussonetia papyrifera
Carya (most)
Catalpa (all)
Cedrela sinensis
Cordyline australis
Eriobotryia japonica
Firmiana simplex
Gevuina avellana
Gymnocladus dioicus

Idesia polycarpa
Juglans (all)
Kalopanax pictus var maximowiczii
Koelreuteria (all)
Laurelia serrata
Lyonothamnus floribundus var asplenifolius
Magnolia (many)
Meliosma veitchiorum
Osmanthus yunnanensis
Paulownia (all)
Phellodendron (all)
Populus lasiocarpa
Populus wilsonii

Pseudopanax arboreum
Pterocarya (all)
Quercus dentata
Rhamnus imeritina
Rhus verniciflua

Sorbus cuspidata
Sorbus sargentiana
Tilia heterophylla var *michauxii*
Trachycarpus fortunei
Zanthoxylum ailanthoides

Cut-leaf (laciniate) foliage

Acer japonicum 'Aconitifolium'
Acer negundo 'Heterophyllum'
Acer palmatum (various)
Acer platanoides (various)
Acer saccharinum (various)
Aesculus hippocastanum laciniata
Alnus (various)
Betula pendula 'Dalecarlica'
Broussonettia papyrifera 'Laciniata'
Caragana arborescens 'Lorbergii'
Carpinus betulus 'Heterophylla'
Castanea sativa (various)
Corylus avellana 'Heterophylla'
Crataegus monogyna 'Pteridifolia'
Fagus sylvatica (various)
Fraxinus excelsior 'Asplenifolia'
Ginkgo biloba 'Laciniata'
Juglans regia 'Laciniata'

Laburnum anagyroides 'Quercifolium'
Morus alba 'Laciniata'
Platanus orientalis var *digitata*
Populus alba 'Paletzkyana'
Prunus avium 'Asplenifolia'
Prunus serotina 'Asplenifolia'
Ptelea trifoliata 'Heterophylla'
Pyrus regelii
Quercus (various)
Rhamnus frangula 'Asplenifolia'
Rhus glabra 'Laciniata'
Rhus typhina 'Laciniata'
Robinia pseudoacacia var *dissecta*
Sambucus (various)
Sorbus aucuparia 'Asplenifolia'
Syringa × *persica* 'Laciniata'
Tilia platyphyllos 'Asplenifolia'
Ulmus glabra 'Crispa'
Vitex negundo 'Incisa'

Variegated foliage

Acanthopanax sieboldianus 'Variegatus'
Acer campestre 'Variegatum'
Acer crataegifolium 'Vietchii'
Acer mono 'Variegatum'
Acer negundo 'Elegans'
Acer negundo 'Variegatum'
Acer platanoides 'Drummondii'
Acer pseudoplatanus (various)
Acer rufinerve 'Albolimbatum'
Aralia (various)
Buxus sempervirens 'Aurea Pendula'
Calocedrus decurrens 'Aureovariegata'
Castanopsis cuspidata 'Variegata'
Catanea sativa 'Albomarginata'
Chamaecyparis lawsoniana (many)
Chamaecyparis nootkatensis 'Aureovariegata'
Cornus controversa 'Variegata'
Cornus mas 'Elegantissima'
Cornus mas 'Variegata'
Crataegus monogyna 'Variegata'
Fagus sylvatica 'Luteovariegata'
Fagus sylvatica 'Tricolor'

Fraxinus ornus 'Variegata'
Fraxinus pensylvanica 'Aucubifolia Variegata'
Ilex (many)
Juniperus (various)
Ligustrum lucidum 'Tricolor'
Liquidambar stryraciflua 'Aureum'
Liriodendron tulipifera 'Aureomarginatum'
Magnolia acuminata 'Aureovariegata'
Picea abies 'Argenteo-spica'
Pinus wallichiana 'Zebrina'
Platanus × *hispanica* 'Suttneri'
Populus × *candicans* 'Aurora'
Quercus cerris 'Variegata'
Quercus robur 'Variegata'
Salix caprea 'Variegata'
Sambucus nigra 'Variegata'
Taxus baccata 'Variegata'
Thuja plicata 'Zebrina'
Thujopsis dolobrata 'Variegata'
Ulmus procera 'Argenteovariegata'
Ulmus × *viminalis* 'Marginata'

Golden or yellow foliage

Acer cappodocicum 'Aureum'
Acer japonicum 'Aureum'
Acer negundo 'Auratum'
Acer pseudoplatanus 'Corstorphinense'
Acer pseudoplatanus 'Worleei'
Acer saccharinum 'Lutescens'
Alnus glutinosa 'Aurea'
Alnus incana 'Aurea'
Catalpa bignonioides 'Aurea'
Cedrus atlantica 'Aurea'

Cedrus deodara 'Aurea'
Cedrus deodara 'Aurea Pendula'
Chamaecyparis (many)
Cornus mas 'Aurea'
Corylus avellana 'Aurea'
Cupressus (various)
Fagus sylvatica 'Aurea Pendula'
Fagus sylvatica 'Zlatia'
Fraxinus excelsior 'Aurea Pendula'
Gleditsia tricanthos 'Sunburst'

Ilex aquifolium 'Flavescens'
Juniperus chinensis 'Aurea'
Laburnum anagyroides 'Aureum'
Laurus nobilis 'Aurea'
Ligustrum lucidum 'Aureum'
Populus alba 'Richardii'
Populus 'Serotina Aurea'
Populus nigra 'Lombardy Gold'
Ptelea trifoliata 'Aurea'
Quercus robur 'Concordia'
Quercus rubra 'Aurea'
Robinia pseudoacacia 'Aurea'
Robinia pseudoacacia 'Frisia'

Sambucus nigra 'Aurea'
Sorbus aria 'Aurea'
Sorbus aria 'Chrysophylla'
Sorbus aucuparia 'Aurea Pendula'
Sorbus aucuparia 'Dirkenii'
Taxus (many)
Thuja (various)
Thujopsis dolobrata 'Aurea'
Tilia × *europaea* 'Wratislaviensis'
Ulmus glabra 'Lutescens'
Ulmus × *hollandica* 'Wredei'
Ulmus procera 'Louis Van Houtte'
Ulmus × *sarniensis* 'Dicksonii'

Grey, white, silvery or bluish foliage

Acacia (various)
Conifers (many)
Elaeagnus augustifolia
Elaeagnus macophylla
Eucalyptus (many)
Halimodendron halodendron
Hippophae rhamnoides
Ilex (various)

Populus alba
Populus canescens
Pyrus × *canescens*
Pyrus elaegrifolia
Pyrus nivalis
Pyrus salicifolia 'Pendula'
Salix alba 'Sericea'
Tilia tomentosa

Reddish and purple foliage

Acer (various)
Betula pendula 'Purple Splendour'
Betula pendula 'Purpurea'
Brachyglottis repanda 'Purpurea'
Carpinus betulus 'Purpurea'
Catalpa × *erubescens* 'Purpurea'
Cercis canadensis 'Forest Pansy'
Corylus avellana 'Purpurea'
Fagus (various)

Gleditsia tricanthos var *inermis* 'Ruby Lace'
Malus (many)
Pittosporum tenuifolium 'Purpureum'
Prunus (many)
Quercus petraea 'Purpurea'
Quercus robur 'Atropurpurea'
Quercus robur 'Fastigiata Purpurea'
Sambucus nigra 'Purpurea'
Ulmus × *sarniensis* 'Purpurea'

Autumn-colouring foliage

Acer (many)
Aesculus (all)
Amelanchier (all)
Betula (many)
Carpinus (all)
Carya (all)
Castanea (various)
Cedrela
Cercidiphyllum
Cercis
Chionanthus
Cladrastis (all)
Cornus (all)
Cotinus
Crataegus (many)
Fagus (all)
Fraxinus (most)
Ginkgo
Gleditsia
Gymnocladus
Hamamelis (all)
Larix (all)
Liquidambar (all)
Liriodendron (all)

Magnolia (various)
Malus (various)
Metasequoia
Nothofagus (various)
Nyssa (all)
Oxydendrum
Parrotia
Phellodendron (most)
Photinia (various)
Picrasma
Populus (various)
Prunus (many)
Pseudolarix
Pyrus (various)
Quercus (many)
Rhus (most)
Salix (various)
Sassafras
Sorbus (many)
Stewartia (all)
Taxodium (all)
Tilia (various)
Ulmus (many)
Zelkova (most)

Ornamental and useful fruit

Abies (most)
Acanthopanax henryi
Acer capillipas
Acer cappadocicum var sinicum
Acer erianthum
Acer pseudoplatanus var erythrocarpum
Acer pseudoplatanus 'Euchlorum'
Acer tataricum
Aesculus (most)
Alnus cordata
Arbutus (various)
Carya (various)
Castanea sativa
Catalpa (various)
Cedrus (all)
Cercis (various)
Clerodendrum trichotomum
Colutea arborescens
Cornus (various)
Corylus (various)
Cotinus coggygria
Cotoneaster (many)
Crataegus (many)
Cydonia oblonga
Diosyrous (various)
Dipteronia sinensis
Elaeagnus umbellata
Eriobotrya japonica
Euodia (various)
Euonymus oxyphyllus
Fraxinus latifolia
Fraxinus mariesii
Fraxinus ornus
Ginkgo biloba (female)
Gleditsia (various)
Gymnocladus dioicus (female)
Heteromeles arbutifolia
Hippophae rhamnoides (female)
Ilex (female)
Juglans regia

Juniperus virginiana 'Glauca'
Koelreuteria paniculata
Ligustrum (various)
Lycium chinense
Maclura pomifera (female)
Magnolia (various)
Malus (many)
Mespilus germanica
Myrica (various)
Ostrya (various)
Paliurus spina-christi
Picea (various)
Pinus (various)
Platanus (various)
Poncirus trifoliata
Prunus (various)
Ptelea trifoliata
Pterocarya (various)
Punica granatum
Pyracanatha atalantioides
Pyrus (various)
Quercus macrolepis
Rehderodendron macrocarpus
Rhamnus (various)
Rhus typhina (female)
Robinia (various)
Sambucus (various)
Sciadopitys verticillata
Sorbus (many)
Staphylea colchica
Stranvaesia davidiana
Symplocos paniculata
Taxus baccata
Taxus baccata 'Lutea'
Tilia (various)
Trachycarpus fortunei
Ulmus glabra
Wienmannia trichosperma
Xanthocerus sorbifolium
Zanthoxylum (various)

Seasons

Winter flowering

Acacia decurrens var dealbata
Buddleia asiatica
Cornus mas
Cornus officinalis
Corylus avellana
Crataegus monogyna 'Biflora'
Garrya elliptica
Hamamelis japonica var arborea
Magnolia campbellii

Parrotia persica
Prunus conradine 'Semiplena'
Prunus dulcis 'Praecox'
Prunus incisa 'February Pink'
Prunus subhirtella 'Autumnalis'
Salix aegyptiaca
Taxus baccata
Ulmus villosa

Late winter flowering

Acer opalus
Acer platanoides
Acer rubrum

Acer saccharinum
Alnus glutinosa
Alnus incana 'Aurea'

Azara microphylla
Camellia reticulata
Corylus chinensis
Corylus colurna
Corylus maxima 'Purpurea'
Fraxinus (various)
Laurus nobilis
Lindera cercidifolia
Magnolia (various)
Parabenzoin praecox
Populus (various)
Prunus × amygdalopersica 'Pollardii'

Prunus armeniaca
Prunus campanulata
Prunus cerasifera
Prunus cerasoides
Prunus conradine
Prunus dulcis
Prunus incisa 'Praecox'
Prunus mume
Pyrus ussuriensis
Salix (many)
Sorbus megalocarpa
Sycopsis sinenisis
Ulmus (most)

Early spring flowering

Acer (various)
Alnus (most)
Amelanchier (most)
Betula (various)
Carpinus (various)
Cornus florida
Cornus nuttallii
Distylum racemosum
Halesia (most)
Hippophae rhamnoides
Magnolia (various)
Paulownia
Phillyrea decora
Photinia serrulata
Picea likiangensis

Prunus 'Accolade'
Prunus avium
Prunus canescens
Prunus cerasifera 'Pissardii'
Prunus cerasus
Prunus domestica
Prunus 'Kursar'
Prunus mahaleb
Prunus padus
Prunus persica
Prunus pseudocerasus 'Cantabrigensis'
Prunus × yedoensis
Pyrus (various)
Quercus (various)
Sorbus meliosmifolia

Spring flowering

Acer spicatum
Adenocarpus decorticans
Aesculus (various)
Arbutus menziesii
Caragana arborescens
Cercis (various)
Cladrastis lutea
Cornus florida
Cotoneaster frigida
Crataegus (many)
Cydonia oblonga
Davidia involucrata
Drimys winteri
Embothrium coccineum
Enkianthus campanulatus
Exochorda (various)
Fraxinus (various)
Ilex (various)
Laburnum (various)

Magnolia (many)
Malus (many)
Maglietia insignis
Mespilus germanica
Parrotiopsis jaquemontiana
Photinia (various)
Pittosporum undulatum
Prunus (various)
Pyracantha atalantioides
Pyrus (most)
Robinia (various)
Sinojackia rehderana
Sophora tetraptera
Sorbus (many)
Staphylea holocarpa
Stranvaesia davidiana
Symplocos paniculata
Syringa vulgaris
Viburnum lentago
Xanthoceras sorbifolium

Summer flowering (including shrubby trees)

Aesculus californica
Aesculus indica
Aesculus parvifolia (shrubby)
Alangium platanifolium
Buddleia alternifolia
Buddleia colvilei
Castanea (various)
Catalpa (various)

Chionanthus retusus
Chionanthus virginicus
Chrysolepis chrysophylla
Cladrastis sinensis
Colutea arborescens
Cornus kousa
Cotinus coggyria
Cotoneaster glaucophyllus var serotina

Erythrina crista-galli
Eugenia myrtifolia
Hoheria (most)
Idesia polycarpa
Koelreuteria paniculata
Laburnum alpinum
Leptospermum scoparium
Ligustrum sinensis
Liriodendron tulipifera
Lonicera quinquelocularis
Maakia (all)
Magnolia (various)
Meliosma (various)
Myricaria germanica
Olearia arborescens
Poliothyrisis sinensis
Pomaderris apetala
Prunus cerasus 'Semperflorens'

Prunus lusitanica
Ptelea trifoliata
Pterocarya (various)
Pterostyrax hispida
Robinia luxurians
Robinia pseudoacacia 'Semperflorens'
Robinia viscosa
Sambucus nigra
Stewartia (most)
Styrax (various)
Syringa pekinensis
Tamarix gallica
Telopea truncata
Tetracentron sinensis
Tilia (most)
Trachycarpus fortunei
Trochydendron aralioides
Weinmannia racemosa

Late summer and autumn flowering (including shrubby trees)

Alnus nitida
Aralia (various)
Arbutus (various)
Buddleia crispa
Calycanthus occidentalis
Catalpa bignonioides
Cedrus (all)
Cephalanthus occidentalis
Clerodendrum (all)
Clethra delavayi
Colletia armata
Colutea arborescens
Cornus macrophylla
Corylus ferox
Elaeagnus macrophylla
Escallonia × exoniensis
Escallonia revoluta
Eucalyptus (various)
Euycryphia (various)
Franklinia altamaha
Fremontodendron californicum
Gordonia axillaris
Hamamelis virginiana
Hibiscus syriacus (various)
Hoheria populnea
Hydrangea dumicola
Hydrangea heteromalia
Hydrangea villosa

Hypericum 'Rowallane'
Itea ilicifolia
Kalopanax pictus
Koelreuteria paniculata
Laburnum anagyroides 'Autumnale'
Lagerstroemia indica
Lavatera olbia
Ligustrum chenaultii
Ligustrum strongylophyllum
Magnolia delavayi
Magnolia grandiflora
Magnolia virginiana
Mahonia acanthifolia
Michelia doltsopa
Myrtus (various)
Nerium oleander
Osmanthus heterophyllus
Oxydendrum arboreum
Paliurus spina-christi
Prunus subhirtella 'Autumnalis'
Punica granatum
Pyracantha augustifolia
Schima wallichii
Sophora japonica
Stewartia (various)
Tilia henryana
Ulmus parviflora
Vitax agnus-castus
Yucca (various)

Soils

Moist or wet soils

Abies (various)
Acer pseudoplatanus
Acer rubrum
Acer saccharinum
Alnus (various)
Amelanchier (various)
Betula × koehnei
Betula nigra

Betula papyrifera
Betula populifolia
Betula pubescens
Calycanthus occidentalis
Cephalanthus occidentalis
Crataegus (various)
Gleditsia aquatica
Hippophae rhamnoides

Leitneria floridana
Liquidambar styraciflua
Magnolia virginiana
Mespilus germanica
Metasequoia glypotostroboides
Myrica (various)
Nyssa sylvatica
Photonia villosa
Picea (various)
Platanus occidentalis
Populus (all)
Pterocarya (various)

Pyrus communis
Quercus bicolor
Quercus falcata
Quercus laurifolia
Quercus nigra
Quercus palustris
Rhamnus frangula
Salix (all)
Sambucus (various)
Sorbus aucuparia
Taxodium distichum
Thuja occidentalis
Ulmus (various)

Clay soils

Abies
Acer
Aesculus
Betula
Carpinus
Chamaecyparis
Cornus
Crataegus
Eucalyptus
Fraxinus
Ilex
Laburnum

Larix
Liriodendron
Malus
Pinus
Populus
Prunus
Pyrus
Quercus
Salix
Sorbus
Taxus
Tilia

Fertile loam soils

Most types of native and ornamental trees

Peaty acid soils

Abies (various)
Acer palmatum
Arbutus (various)
Betula (various)
Clethra barbinervis
Cornus florida
Enkianthus campanulatus
Halesia monticola
Laurus nobilis

Magnolia (various)
Myrica cerifera
Nyssa sylvatica
Oxydendrum arboreum
Populus (various)
Quercus (various)
Rhododendron arboreum
Salix (various)
Stewartia (various)
Styrax (various)

Sandy and gravelly soils

Acer decurrens var dealbata
Acer negundo
Acer pseudoplatanus
Ailanthus altissima
Albizia julibrissen
Alnus incana
Amelanchier (various)
Betula (all)
Broussonetia papyrifera
Caragana arborescens
Carpinus (various)
Castanea (all)
Cercidiphyllum japonicum
Cercis (all)
Cladrastis lutea
Clerodendrum trichotomum
Crataegus (all)
Cupressus (various)

Cydonia oblonga
Eucalyptus (various)
Fraxinus (various)
Gleditsia (all)
Halimodendron halodendron
Ilex (all)
Juniperus (all)
Koelreuteria paniculata
Ligustrum (various)
Maclura pomifera
Pinus (various)
Platanus (various)
Populus (various)
Quercus agrifolia
Quercus cerris
Quercus ilex
Quercus marilandica
Quercus petraea

Quercus robur
Quercus rubra
Robinia (all)
Salix (various)
Sambucus (various)

Sassafras albidum
Sophora japonica
Sorbus aucuparia
Tamarix gallica
Tilia (various)
Ulmus (various)

Very dry soils

Ailanthus altissima
Alnus incana
Betula pendula
Betula populifolia
Caragana arborescens
Celtis (various)
Cercis (various)
Elaeagnus augustifolia
Gleditsia triacanthos

Halimodendron halodendron
Hippophae rhamnoides
Juniperus (all)
Pinus (various)
Robinia pseudoacacia
Sambucus (various)
Tamarix gallica
Ulmus parviflora
Ulmus pumila

Alkaline or chalk soils

Abies cephalonica
Abies cilicia
Abies pinsapo
Acer campestre
Acer negundo
Acer platanoides
Acer pseudoplatanus
Aesculus (most)
Arbutus andrachne
Arbutus unedo
Buxus (all)
Carpinus (most)
Cedrus (all)
Cercis siliquastrum
Cornus mas
Cotoneaster (most)
Crataegus (various)
× *Cupressocyparis*
Euonymus (various)
Fagus (various)
Fraxinus (various)
Hibiscus syriacus
Juglans regia
Juniperus (various)
Larix (various)

Laurus nobilis
Ligustrum (various)
Maclura pomifera
Malus (various)
Morus nigra
Photinia serrulata
Picea omorika
Pinus nigra
Populus alba
Prunus avium
Prunus lusitanica
Quercus canariensis
Quercus frainetto
Quercus ilex
Rhus (various)
Salix (various)
Sambucus (various)
Sorbus aria
Syringa vulgaris
Taxus (various)
Thuja (various)
Thujopsis dolabrata
Ulmus (all)
Yucca (various)
Zelkova cretica

Climatic Conditions

Mild climate (including shrubby trees)

Acacia
Albizia
Ardisia
Aristotelia
Atherosperma
Azara
Banksia
Bauhinia
Callistemon
Cassia
Cercocarpus
Cinnomomum
Citharexylum
Cleyera

Cordyline
Crinodendron
Datura
Drimys
Elaeocarpus
Embothrium
Entelea
Eriobotrya
Erythrina
Eucalyptus
Eugenia
Feijoa
Firmiana
Fremontodendron

Garrya	Olea
Gevuina	Paliurus
Gordonia	Parkinsonia
Grewia	Persea
Griselinia	Peumus
Hakea	Phytolacca
Hoheria	Pistacia
Idesia	Pittosporum
Itea	Plagianthus
Lagerstroemia	Planera
Laurelia	Poncirus
Laurus	Prostranthera
Leitneria	Pseudopanax
Leptospermum	Punica
Lithocarpus	Quillaia
Lomatia	Reevesia
Lyonothamnus	Rehderodendron
Machilus	Schima
Manglietia	Schinus
Melalenca	Sparmannia
Melia	Sutherlandia
Meterosideros	Telopea
Michelia	Ternstroemia
Myoporum	Tibouchina
Mytus	Villaresia
Neolitsea	Vitex
Nerium	Weinmannia
Notelaea	Xylosma

Very sunny conditions

Caragana	Halimodendron
Celtis	Hibiscus
Cercis	Hippophae
Clerodendrum	Juniperus
Cotinus	Leptospermum
Crataegus	Paliurus
Elaeagnus (deciduous)	Pinus
Erythrina	Robinia
Gleditsia	Tamarix

Shaded conditions

Acer palmatum	Laurus
Azara	Ligustrum
Buxus	Magnolia
Camellia	Osmanthus
Cephalotaxus	Phillyrea
Corylus	Podocarpus
Cotoneaster	Prunus lauroceras
Drimys	Prunus lustianica
Elaeagnus (evergreen)	Rhododendron
Fagus	Sambucus
Ilex	Taxus
Laurelia	Tsuga

Windy conditions

Acer platanoides	Ilex aquifolium
Acer pseudoplatanus	Pinus nigra
Alnus glutinosa	Platanus × hispanica
Carpinus betulus	Populus alba
Crataegus monogyna	Populus canescens
Fraxinus excelsior	Populus nigra

Prunus spinosa
Quercus robur
Sambucus nigra

Taxus baccata
Tilia × europaea
Ulmus glabra

Salty coastal conditions

Acacia decurrens var *dealbata*
Acer campestre
Acer pseudoplatanus
Ailanthus altissima
Amelanchier lamarckii
Arbutus unedo
Castanea sativa
Cordyline australis
Crataegus monogyna
Cryptomeria japonica
Cupressus macrocarpa
Elaeagnus augustifolia
Eucalyptus gunnii
Euonymus fortunei
Ficus carica
Fraxinus excelsior
Hippophae rhamnoides
Ilex aquifolium
Juniperus virginiana
Laburnum anagyroides
Laurus nobilis
Ligustrum lucidum
Magnolia grandiflora
Phillyrea latifolia
Pinus contorta

Pinus nigra var *maritima*
Pinus pinaster
Pinus radiata
Pinus strobus
Pinus thunbergii
Pittosporum tennifolium
Platanus × hispanica
Populus alba
Populus (hybrids)
Prunus serotina
Prunus spinosa
Quercus cerris
Quercus ilex
Quercus robur
Rhamnus alaternus
Robinia pseudoacacia
Salix alba
Sambucus nigra
Sophora japonica
Sorbus aucuparia
Tamarix gallica
Trachycarpus fortunei
Ulmus augustifolia var *cornubensis*
Ulmus glabra
Ulmus × sarniensis

Selection for Various Uses and Sites

Fast growing

Abies alba
Abies grandis
Abies procera
Acacia decurrens var *dealbata*
Acer macrophyllum
Acer palmatum
Acer pseudoplatanus
Aesculus hippocastanum
Ailanthus althissima
Alnus glutinosa
Aralia chinensis
Eucalyptus (various)
Fraxinus excelsior
Ilex × altaclarensis
Koelreuteria paniculata
Laburnum anagyroides
Larix decidua
Liquidambar styraciflua
Liriodendron tulipifera
Magnolia acuminata
Malus (various)
Metasequoia glyptostroboides

Nothofagus obliqua
Picea (many)
Pinus (many)
Populus (all)
Prunus avium
Prunus laurocerasus
Pseudotsuga menziesii
Pyrus communis
Quercus canariensis
Quercus cerris
Quercus macranthera
Quercus rubra
Quercus velutina
Salix alba
Sequoia sempervirens
Sequoiadendron giganteum
Sorbus aucuparia
Thuja plicata
Tilia × europaea
Tsuga heterophylla
Ulmus procera
Zelkova carpinifolia

Soil stabilising

Acer pseudoplatanus
Aesculus parviflora
Ailanthus altissima

Alnus incana
Caragana arborescens
Clerodendrum trichotomum

135

Corylus avellana
Cotoneaster frigidus
Crataegus monogyna
Elaeagnus augustifolia
Fraxinus excelsior
Gleditsia triacanthos
Hippophae rhamnoides
Pinus nigra
Populus alba
Prunus cerasifera

Pterocarya fraxinifolia
Quercus cerris
Rhamnus cathartica
Rhus typhina
Robinia pseudoacacia
Salix fragilis
Sorbus aria
Sorbus aucuparis
Syringa vulgaris
Tilia × europaea
Ulmus procera

Shelter belt and screens

Abies alba
Acer campestre
Acer pseudoplatanus
Aesculus hippocastanum
Alnus glutinosa
Betula pendula
Buxus sempervirens
Castanea sativa
Cedrus deodara
Chamaecyparis lawsoniana
Corylus avellana
Cotoneaster frigidus
Crataegus monogyna
Crataegus oxyacantha
Crataegus prunifolia
Cryptomeria japonica
× Cupressocyparis leylandii
Cupressus macrocarpa
Fagus sylvatica
Fraxinus excelsior
Fraxinus ornus
Hippophae rhamnoides
Ilex aquifolium
Larix decidua
Larix kaempferi
Malus sylvestris
Nothofagus obliqua
Nothofagus procera

Picea abies
Picea sitchensis
Pinus contorta
Pinus nigra
Pinus radiata
Pinus sylvestris
Populus nigra 'Italica'
Populus 'Robusta'
Populus 'Serotina'
Prunus avium
Prunus cerasifera
Prunus laurocerasus
Prunus lusitanica
Prunus padus
Prunus spinosa
Pyrus communis
Quercus cerris
Quercus ilex
Quercus robur
Quercus rubra
Salix alba
Sambucus nigra
Sorbus aria
Sorbus aucuparia
Tilia × europaea
Tsuga canadensis
Ulmus procera
Viburnum opulus

Field hedges

Acer campestre
Carpinus betulus
Corylus avellana
Crataegus monogyna
Fagus sylvatica
Ilex aquifolium

Pinus sylvestris
Prunus spinosa
Salix caprea
Tilia × europaea
Ulmus procera
Viburnum lantana

Clipped hedges for gardens

Buxus sempervirens
Carpinus betulus
Cedrus deodara
Chamaecyparis lawsoniana
Corylus avellana
Cotoneaster simonsii
Crataegus monogyna
× Cupressocyparis leylandii
Escallonia macrantha
Fagus sylvatica

Hippophae rhamnoides
Ilex aquifolium
Laurus nobilis
Ligustrum vulgare
Lonicera nitida
Nothofagus obliqua
Prunus laurocerasus
Prunus lusitanica
Taxus baccata
Thuja plicata
Tsuga heterophylla

Informal flowering hedges for gardens

Many flowering shrubs and shrubby trees, for example *Berberis, Cotoneaster, Rhododendron*

Hedgerow trees

Acer campestre
Acer platanoides
Acer pseudoplatanus
Alnus glutinosa
Betula pendula
Carpinus betulus
Castanea sativa
Fagus sylvatica
Fraxinus excelsior
Ilex aquifolium
Juglans regia
Nothofagus obliqua

Pinus nigra
Pinus sylvestris
Populus canescens
Prunus avium
Quercus cerris
Quercus petraea
Quercus robur
Salix alba
Tilia cordata
Tilia × europaea
Tilia platyphyllos
Ulmus glabra

Forestry crops

Abies alba
Abies grandis
Abies procera
Acer pseudoplatanus
Alnus glutinosa
Betula pendula
Carpinus betulus
Castanea sativa
Cedrus deodara
Chamaecyparis lawsoniana
Corylus avellana
Cryptomeria japonica
Fagus sylvatica
Fraxinus excelsior
Ilex aquifolium
Larix decidua
Larix × eurolepis
Larix kaempfera

Nothofagus obliqua
Picea abies
Picea sitchensis
Pinus (various)
Populus (various)
Prunus avium
Pseudotsuga menziesii
Quercus petraea
Quercus robur
Quercus rubra
Salix 'Caerulea'
Salix viminalis
Sequoia sempervirens
Sequoiadendron giganteum
Taxus baccata
Thuja plicata
Tilia cordata
Tsuga heterophylla
Ulmus glabra

Amenity woodland and wildlife conservation areas

Native and naturalised trees and shrubs (see list)
Fruiting shrubs suitable for animal food plants (below)

Berberis vulgaris
Cornus sanguinea
Cotoneaster simonsii
Euonymus europaeus
Gautheria shallon
Hypericum audrosaemum
Lecesteria formosa
Ligustrum vulgare
Lonicera xylosteum
Prunus spinosa

Rhamnus cathartica
Rhamnus frangula
Ribes nigrum
Rosa canina
Sorbus rupicola
Symphoricarpos albus
Vaccinium vitis-idaea
Viburnum lantana
Viburnum opulus

Motorway planting

Amenity woodland and wildlife conservation areas (see list) (all)
Forestry crop plants (see list) (various)
Native and naturalised trees and shrubs (see list) (all)

Trees suitable for arboreta, botanic gardens and stately homes
(selection of exotic ornamental trees useful as single specimens, groups or avenues)

Abies magnifica
Acer macrophyllum
Aesculus indica
Ailanthus altissima
Alnus cordata
Araucaria araucana
Arbutus menziesii
Betula maximowicziana
Calocedrus decurrens
Carpinus laxiflora
Carya tomentosa
Castanea mollissima
Catalpa speciosa
Cedrus libani
Cercidiphyllum japonicum
Cercis canadensis
Chamaecyparis nootkatensis
Cornus controversa
Corylus chinensis
Cotinus obovatus
Crataegus molli
Cryptomeria japonica
Cunninghamia lanceolata
Cupressus sempervirens
Davidia involucrata
Diospyros lotus
Ehretia dicksonii
Eucalyptus dalrymplena
Euoidia hupehenis
Fraxinus latifolia
Ginkgo latifolia
Gleditsia sinensis
Gymnocladus dioicus
Halesia monticola
Idesia polycarpa
Ilex diprena
Juglans nigra
Juniperus virginiana
Koelreuteria paniculata

Larix kaempferi
Liquidambar styraciflua
Liriodendron tulipifera
Maclura pomifera
Magnolia campbellii
Malus trilobata
Metasequoia glyptostroboides
Morus nigra
Nothofagus dombeyi
Nyssa sylvatica
Ostrya japonica
Oxydendrum arboreum
Paulownia tomentosa
Phellodendron lavallei
Picea smithiana
Pinus wallichiana
Platanus orientalis
Podocarpus salignus
Populus maximowiczii
Prunus serrula
Pseudolarix amabilis
Pseudotsuga menziesii
Pterocarya fraxinifolia
Salix × chrysocoma
Sassafras albidum
Sciadopitys verticillata
Sequoia sempervirens
Sequoiadendron giganteum
Sorbus sargentiana
Sophora japonica
Stewartia sinensis
Styrax obassia
Taxodium distichum
Thuja plicata
Tilia petiolaris
Tsuga mertensiana
Ulmus villosa
Umbellularia californica
Zelkova carpinifolia

Industrial areas and land reclamation

Acer campestre
Acer negundo
Acer platanoides
Acer pseudoplatanus
Aesculus hippocastanum
Ailanthus altissima
Alnus cordata
Alnus glutinosa
Alnus incana
Alnus viridis
Amelanchier lamarkii
Betula pendula
Betula pubescens
Buxus sempervirens
Caprinus betulus
Castanea sativa
Cotoneaster × watereri
Crataegus (various)

Fraxinus excelsior
Gleditsia triacanthos
Hippophae rhamnoides
Ilex × altaclarensis
Ilex aquifolium
Laburnum anagyroides
Larix decidua
Ligustrum sinense
Malus (various)
Mespilus germanica
Morus nigra
Phillyrea latifolia
Pinus nigra
Platanus × hispanica
Populus (various)
Prunus (various)
Pterocarya fraxinifolia
Pterocarya stenoptera

Pyrus communis
Pyrus nivalis
Pyrus salicifolia
Quercus cerris
Quercus × hispanica
Quercus ilex
Quercus robur
Quercus rubra
Rhus typhina
Robinia pseudoacacia
Salix (various)

Sambucus nigra
Sorbus (various)
Staphylea colchica
Syringa vulgaris
Tilia cordata
Tilia × euchlora
Tilia × europaea
Tilia platyphyllos
Ulmus procera
Viburnum opulus

Towns

Town gardens, new housing estates and city landscape schemes

Acer capillipes
Acer cappadocicum
Acer negundo (and cultivars)
Acer palmatum (and cultivars)
Acer platanoides (and cultivars)
Acer pseudoplatanus var purpurea
Acer rubrum
Aesculus × carnea
Aesculus indica
Aesculus pavia
Alnus cordata
Alnus incana (and cultivars)
Alnus viridis
Amelanchier canadensis
Amelanchier lamarkii
Aralia chinensis
Arbutus unedo
Betula ermanii
Betula lutea
Betula papyrifera
Betula pendula (cultivars)
Betula utilis
Buxus sempervirens
Caragana arborescens
Carpinus betulus 'Fastigiata'
Castanea sativa 'Variegata'
Catalpa bignonioides
Chamaecyparis lawsoniana (cultivars)
Chaemaecyparis pisifera (cultivars)
Clerodendrum trichotomum
Cornus controversa
Cornus florida
Cornus mas
Corylus avellana (cultivars)
Cotoneaster (various)
Crataegus crus-galli
Crataegus monogyna (cultivars)
Crataegus phaenopyrum
Crataegus prunifolia
Cryptomeria japonica 'Elegans'
× Cupressocyparis leylandii
Cupressus glabra 'Pyramidalis'
Cupressus macrocarpa 'Donards Gold'
Cydonia oblonga
Davidia involucrata
Elaeagnus augustifolia

Fagus sylvatica var heterophylla
Fraxinus excelsior 'Jaspidea'
Fraxinus ornus
Fraxinus oxycarpa 'Raywood'
Gleditsia triacanthos 'Bujoti'
Gleditsia triancanthos 'Sunburst'
Hippophae rhamnoides
Ilex aquifolium (cultivars)
Koelreuteria paniculata
+ Laburnocytisus adamii
Laurus nobilis
Ligustrum lucidum
Liquidambar styraciflua
Magnolia salicifolia
Magnolia × soulangiana
Magnolia × veitchii
Malus (cultivars)
Mespilus germanica
Morus alba
Morus nigra
Nothofagus antarctica
Nothofagus dombeyi
Nyssa sylvatica
Ostry japonica
Oxydendrum arboreum
Parrotia persica
Phillyrea latifolia
Picea omorika
Pinus parviflora
Pinus pinea
Podocarpus audinus
Populus alba
Prunus (cultivars)
Pyrus (cultivars)
Quercus coccinea
Quercus palustris
Quercus phellos
Rhus typhina
Robinia pseudoacacia 'Frisia'
Robinia pseudoacacia 'Inermis'
Salix agyptiaca
Sophora japonica
Sorbus (cultivars)
Thuja plicata 'Zebrina'
Tilia × euchlora
Tilia mongolica

Tilia platyphyllos 'Rubra'
Tsuga mertensiana

Umbellularia californica
Zelkova sinica

Roadway planting

Wide

Acer campestre
Acer cappadocicum
Acer × lobelii
Acer platanoides 'Columnare'
Acer pseudoplatanus 'Erectum'
Acer saccharum 'Monumentale'
Aesculus × carnea
Ailanthus altissima
Alnus cordata
Alnus glutinosa 'Pyramidalis'
Carpinus betulus 'Fastigiata'
Carpinus prunifolia
Fraxinus excelsior 'Jaspidea'
Ginkgo biloba
Gleditsia triacanthos
Ligustrum luncidum

Liriodendron tulipifera 'Fastigiata'
Nothofagus obliqua
Ostrya virginiana
Platanus × hispanica
Prunus avium
Prunus padus
Prunus serotina
Quercus coccinea
Quercus palustris
Quercus robur 'Fastigiata'
Salix 'Caerulea'
Sophora japonica
Sorbus domestica
Sorbus terminalis
Tilia cordata 'Swedish Upright'

Narrow

Acer rubrum 'Scanlon'
Acer rufinerve
Alnus viridis
Carpinus betulus 'Columnaris'
Crataegus mongyna 'Stricta'
Fraxinus oxycarpa 'Raywood'
Laburnum × watereri 'Vossii'
Malus tschonoskii
Prunus × hillieri 'Spire'

Prunus sargentii
Prunus 'Umineko'
Pyrus calleryana 'Chanticleer'
Pyrus communis 'Beech Hill'
Robinia pseudoacacia 'Inermis'
Sorbus aria 'Lutescens'
Sorbus aucuparia 'Fastigiata'
Sorbus 'Sheerwater Seedling'
Sorbus × thuringiaca 'Fastigiata'

Parks and recreational areas (a selection of large trees)

Abies procera
Acer pseudoplatanus
Aesculus hippocastanum
Ailanthus altissima
Betula pendula
Carpinus betulus
Castanea sativa
Catalpa speciosa
Cedrus libani
Chamaecyparis lawsoniana
Cryptomeria japonica
Eucalyptus gunnii
Fagus sylvatica
Fraxinus excelsior
Juglans nigra
Larix decidua

Liriodendron tulipifera
Nothofagus procera
Picea abies
Pinus sylvestris
Populus nigra 'Italica'
Pseudotsuga menziesii
Quercus ilex
Robinia pseudoacacia
Salix alba
Sequoia sempervirens
Sequoiadendron giganteum
Taxus baccata
Thuja plicata
Tilia cordata
Tsuga canadensis
Ulmus glabra

Checklist of Latin and Common English Names

Latin Generic Name	Common English Name
Abies	silver fir
Acer	maples and sycamore
Aesculus	horse chestnut
Ailanthus	tree of heaven
Alnus	alder
Araucaria	monkey puzzle
Arbutus	strawberry tree
Betula	birch
Buxus	box
Carpinus	hornbeam
Castanea	sweet chestnut
Catalpa	Indian bean tree
Cedrus	cedar
Cercis	Judas tree
Chamaecyparis	false cypress
Cornus	dogwood
Crataegus	hawthorn
Cupressocyparis	Leyland cypress
Cupressus	cypress
Eucalyptus	gum tree
Fagus	beech
Fraxinus	ash
Hamamelis	witch hazel
Hippophae	sea buckthorn
Ilex	holly
Juglans	walnut
Juniperus	juniper
Larix	larch
Laurus	bay
Liquidambar	sweet gum
Liriodendron	tulip tree
Malus	apples and crab apples
Metasequoia	dawn redwood
Morus	mulberry
Nothofagus	southern beech
Picea	spruce
Pinus	pine
Platanus	plane
Populus	poplar
Prunus	cherry, peach and plum
Pyrus	pear
Quercus	oak
Robinia	acacia
Salix	willow
Sambucus	elder
Sequoia	Californian redwood
Sequoiadendron	Wellingtonia
Sorbus	rowan or mountain ash, whitebeam
Syringa	lilac
Taxodium	swamp cypress
Taxus	yew
Tilia	lime
Ulmus	elm

Index

Page numbers in **bold** type denote plates; page numbers in *italics* denote figures